I0139458

COLLEGE STATION, TEXAS
1938/1988

by

Deborah Lynn Balliew

"College Station, Texas 1938/1988" by Deborah Lynn Balliew. ISBN 978-1-62137-991-1 (softcover).

Published 2017 by Virtualbookworm.com Publishing Inc., P.O.Box 9949, College Station, TX, 77842, US.

©2017 Deborah Lynn Balliew. All rights reserved. No part of this publication may be reproduced, stored in a retrieval system, or transmitted in any form or by any means, electronic, mechanical, recording or otherwise, without the prior written permission of Deborah Lynn Balliew.

For

TIMOTHY ROBERT McWILLIAMS

My precious brother whom my family and I dearly miss

Table of Contents

Acknowledgments

A WORD OF GRATITUDE is due to the College Station City Council which made this rewarding experience available to me and generously funded the project. Mayor Gary Halter and Councilwoman Patricia Boughton especially showed continued interest in the history and were always willing to answer my questions. City staff members Karen Dickson, Shane Dillard, Dian Jones, and particularly, Pamela Piner Jones and Janis Schwartz provided enthusiastic encouragement. I cannot adequately thank Jan for her kindness and support. She not only spent late nights typing the thesis and transcribing the interviews, but she also assured me that she would be there when I needed any help.

I am indebted to Jeffrey P. Balliew for his constant support and for traveling 800 miles to reproduce photographs appearing in the thesis. Without his expertise and generous effort, I surely would not have been able to provide illustrations with this study. I would also like to thank my family, especially my mother, who always kept me in their prayers.

My sincerest appreciation is extended to Dr. Herbert H. Lang, Professor of History at Texas A&M University, for his guidance in directing this research. He provided latitude that I might learn through this experience and offered perceptive suggestions and corrections that greatly enhanced this manuscript. I am also grateful to Dr. Claude H. Hall and Dr. Melvin C. Schroeder who served on my graduate committee.

Publication of the book has been supported by the City of College Station and the Historic Preservation Committee. Committee members include Lois Beach, Paul Van Riper, Peggy Owens, Norma Teets, John Paul Abbott, Maggie McGraw, Patricia Boughton and Gary Halter, Chairman. Their efforts and those persons who contributed photographs are much appreciated.

Deborah L. Balliew

Introduction

EACH CITY, molded by the events and circumstances of its past, develops an individual identity, yet cannot remain isolated from other political entities. It interacts with other governmental and social institutions, profoundly affecting its neighbors in surrounding areas as well as contributing to the total national urban experience. Scholars recently turned their attention to the study of the growth, nature, and influence of cities in America. Professional historians began to analyze the development of individual cities when the 1920 Census disclosed that the United States was, for the first time, predominantly urban.

The mushroom growth of American cities in the early 1900s was the result of an urban trend that began soon after the Civil War. The profound economic developments of the post-war era stimulated the expansion of existing cities and led to the establishment of new ones. The use of modern farm machinery, a manifestation of the Agricultural Revolution, vastly increased the output of agricultural goods, but also displaced many farmers who were compelled to find work in the industries of the burgeoning cities. The railroads facilitated the movement of raw materials and food across the nation, and thus encouraged large scale manufacturing and the evolution of national markets. This phenomenon of urban growth in the United States coincided with world-wide change on a vast scale. The mechanization of agriculture and the opening up of fertile farming areas in the American West, Argentina, and Australia along with urbanization prompted Old World farmers to migrate to areas affording opportunity.

Many Americans, their ideas shaped by their rural heritage, viewed the increase in the number and size of cities with suspicion. The United States had always been an agricultural nation. The founding fathers stressed the importance and advantages of an agrarian society. They believed that agriculture was economically essential to the developing country, and that the discipline of farming Individually-owned land would forge a proper American national character. Urban life, as they knew it in Europe, eroded the common man's foundation of virtue and freedom. Thomas Jefferson, an ardent opponent of large cities, wrote, " I think our governments will remain virtuous for many centuries as long as they are chiefly agricultural, and this will be as long as there shall be vacant lands in any part of America. When they get piled upon one another in large cities, as in Europe, they will become corrupt as in Europe."

Influenced by this rural-agricultural tradition, the American people perceived the rise of the city as a challenge to fundamental American values. The emphasis by city dwellers on economic gain and the increase of mechanization in industries produced an atmosphere of sterility and impersonality. A lonely existence amid a crowd, characterized urban lifestyle. Mark Twain referred to New York as "a splendid desert — a domed and steepled solitude, where a stranger is lonely in the midst of a million of his race." Although criticism never abated, cities expanded and multiplied. By the late 1800s the industrial city had become an integral part of the American system.

As the United States became ever more urbanized, the need to comprehend the complexities, characteristics, and potential of cities increased proportionately. In the 19th century, leaders had little experience with urban growth. The individual city burgeoned without constraints, and new problems, unique to urban life, arose. Officials, possessing only a vague awareness of their own city's history and without precedence for referral, experimented with sometimes bizarre solutions to problems. Their inconsistent efforts and the lack of orderliness in city development did little to further improvement of conditions. Charles Glaab, in *The American City: A Documentary History*, described these efforts and the uneasiness that they produced. He wrote, "Each city, large and small, is like a palimpsest, marked with hasty erasures, corrections, rebuilding, and redirection. Each city is the sum of its history. We become aware of this not primarily from any sense of sentimental tradition or local loyalty, but from the friction of daily urban life."

One of the keys to understanding the mechanisms of a modern city is to have an appreciation for its history. The knowledge of how the fragments that make up a city's life pieced together illuminates the way it developed and the manner in which it did. History provides a basis by which past growth can be scrutinized and effective policies can be formulated. While most civic leaders strive ultimately to achieve similar goals and have comparable priorities, a city is the product of its unique circumstances and of the activities and ideas of the particular people who comprise its citizenry. The distinctive character of each city evolves because a city is the product of human nature.

The growth of the City of College Station, Texas is analogous in many ways to the growth of other American cities. Yet, College Station has encountered incidents vastly different from the normal urban experiences. The city's inception occurred with the establishment of the Agricultural and Mechanical College of Texas, and the location of the A&M College can be attributed in good measure to the work of the citizens of Bryan, Texas. Thus, the history of Texas A&M University and Bryan are inextricably mixed with the history of College Station. The prime purpose of this study is to provide a history of the city of College Station. But, more than a recital of historic records, the intent is to explain how the city developed, what events shaped its character, and what influenced its leaders to govern the city as they did. This study, it is hoped, will also provide a means to evaluate the past and to direct future endeavors.

.

Chapter I

Before the City

BRAZOS COUNTY IS DELTA-SHAPED, outlined by the Brazos River to the west and by the Navasota River to the east. The confluence of the two rivers marks the southern tip of the county, and the Old San Antonio Road delineates the northern boundary. Anglo-American colonization of this part of Texas did not begin until the 1840s. Other cultures had previously utilized the land, but none had established permanent residence.

Indians periodically inhabited what is now Brazos County. They were the friendly, semi-nomadic Wichita tribes, the Tawakonis and the Wacos, and the nomadic Tonkawas. Several of these tribes lived throughout Central Texas, and the Wichitas ranged as far north as Kansas.[1] The semi-agricultural Tawakonis and the Wacos cultivated corn, squash, and beans and constructed underground granaries to preserve seeds. The men of the tribes hunted buffalo in the area comprising present-day Brazos, Robertson, Milam, Limestone, and Grimes counties until the Comanches and the Cherokees invaded their hunting grounds in the late 1700s.[2] The first American settlers coexisted peacefully with the Tawakonis, Wacos, and the Tonkawas, but often encountered trouble with the Comanches.

For approximately 300 years, Texas belong to the Spanish empire. Although the Spaniards never colonized the Brazos County area, Spanish explorers, officials, and citizens frequently moved through the region. In 1542 Luis de Moscoso de Alvarado attempted to lead Hernando de Soto's men from the Arkansas River, the place of de Soto's death, to Spanish settlements in northern Mexico. Historians suggest that Moscoso reached the place where the Brazos River crosses the Old San Antonio Road before he turned back.[3] Domingo Teran de los Rios, the first provincial governor of Texas, blazed El Camino Real or the Old San Antonio Road in 1691 with the purpose of establishing a direct route from Monclava, the capital of the province, to the missions in East Texas. The route developed into the major thoroughfare of Spanish Texas. Consequently, most early Texan travelers passed along what later became the northern boundary of Brazos County. Moses Austin used this road in 1820 when he journeyed to San Antonio to ask the Spanish governor for permission to settle Anglo-American families in Texas.[4]

The Spanish government granted Moses Austin the right to settle 300 families in Texas, but Austin died before he saw his dream brought to fruition. His son, Stephen F. Austin, promised his father that he would carry on the colonization plans. The younger Austin traveled across Texas from Nacogdoches in the northeast to La Bahia along the coast searching for a suitable area to settle colonists. He was most impressed with the region south of the Old San Antonio Road lying between the Colorado and the Brazos Rivers.5 Austin began bringing people into Texas in the fall of 1821. That year Robert Millican established the first Anglo-American settlement in the Brazos County area.6 In 1824, he received title to two-and-one-half leagues of land centered around the present town of Millican. Most of Austin's first settlers, however, chose homesites in areas further south.

Richard Carter and his family, from Morgan County, Alabama, were among the last group of colonists introduced by Stephen F. Austin. In 1831 Carter received a league of land from the Mexican government, and by October of that year, had erected a house on Saline Creek, later renamed Carter Creek, two miles east of the present Texas A&M University. Thus, Richard Carter became College Station's earliest resident. His land grant encompassed much of what is College Station today.7

People living between the Navasota and Brazos rivers in the early 1830s were most troubled by sporadic attacks of Comanches and other hostile Indians. James Dunn and Eleazer Wheelock built homes that also served as fortifications, and Parker Fort was constructed in 1834 at the headwaters of the Navasota.8 Settlers raised a company of fifty men to fight Indian raiders. The Indians, however, did not represent the only danger. Mexican troops moved through the area in pursuit of rebellious Texas patriots who were assembled southeast of the county. To avoid the Mexicans and hostile Indians, the families, including the Carters, retreated to the forts in 1835 and remained there until Texas won its independence in 1836.

The 1840s ushered in an era of increased prosperity for residents in the area that continued until the Civil War. The creation of Brazos County was one of the first major achievements of that period. In 1837 Washington County had been organized. It originally included all the land between the Brazos and the Navasota rivers and the area southwest of the junction of the two rivers. People in that part now included in Brazos County became dissatisfied with their initial local government. For one thing, the county seat, Mount Vernon, was fifty miles away, and to reach it required the crossing of the Brazos River which was almost impassible for as much as six months of the year. On January 13, 1841, citizens residing between the two rivers petitioned for the creation of a new county.9 By an Act of the Congress of the Republic of Texas on January 30, 1841, that part of Washington County lying between the Brazos and the Navasota rivers became Navasota County. A government was organized in the spring, and by October 1841 the town of Boonville, named in honor of settler Mordecai Boon, was designated the county seat. At the next session of Congress in January 1842, the name "Brazos" was substituted for Navasota. The reason for making this change remains unclear.10

Most of the inhabitants of the newly formed county were engaged in raising crops. Some residents, however, began capturing wild cattle for a distant market — an activity that was a prototype of the cattle industry that developed after the Civil War. The women provided the basic amenities of civilization and were hospitable to the increasing number of travelers passing through the county. Sam Houston was one of the numerous guests that Mrs. Carter accommodated during those early years.11 Social gatherings among the women were not only popular but necessary because amidst the wilderness surroundings, they afforded one of the few links to civilization. In 1879 Kate Efnor, in her historical sketch of Brazos County, wrote that the ladies "being cut off from all intercourse with the outside fashionable world, were fertile in expedients to establish and maintain the highest possible degree of sociability among themselves..."[12] Quilting bees were attended by women living as much as fifteen to twenty miles away.

Early settlers were indeed fortunate in the amount and variety of natural resources in Brazos County. A comfortable lifestyle could be sustained by utilizing the abundant wildlife and native vegetation. Large herds of wild horses and cattle roamed the area, and wild game such as deer, bear, javelina, turkey, quail, and prairie chicken abounded. Men came from great distances to hunt. One man from Washington County even referred to Brazos County as his "poultry yard."[13] Women filled their aprons with eggs laid by the prairie chickens in the open fields. Using the bounteous indigenous fruits — blackberries, dewberries, wild plums, strawberries, persimmons, grapes, and red haws, they preserved jellies and jams and made wine.[14]

Water was one of the few resources that was not always to be found in abundance. There were only a few wells that could be counted on. Most families took up land along rivers or creeks in order to be assured of an adequate water supply. But even the creeks that flowed did so intermittently, and it was not unusual for farmers to haul water five or six miles.[15]

One active member of the region, Harvey Mitchell, began his career in Brazos County as a school teacher. A native of Tennessee, Mitchell soon became involved in county politics. He was elected to various local offices and participated in a myriad of activities. He later played a major role in the establishment of the Agricultural and Mechanical College of Texas in the county. His influence penetrated so many aspects of community life that he became known as the "Father of Brazos County."[16]

The Carter family returned to their one-room log cabin on Carter Creek in December 1841, and Carter developed a prosperous farm and ranching operation. In the 1850 Census, Carter listed his occupation as farmer, and reported that he owned 350 head of cattle, five horses, and five slaves. At that time only three other Brazos County residents owned more cattle.[17]

Using Negro slaves to manage the cattle, Carter expanded his ranching operation. The slaves' duties included the rounding up of the cattle for branding and driving them to Galveston where they were shipped to New Orleans. Although there was only a limited market for Texas cattle before the Civil War, Carter's wealth multiplied. The 1860 Census revealed that he owned 1000 head of cattle, thirty-one horses, and twenty-two slaves. He was considered to be one of the top cotton and corn producers in the county. Between 1846 and 1860, Carter's estate had increased from $5800 to $30,000. Much of this increase may be ascribed to an increase in the value of land and cattle. The most significant factor, however, was the increased value of slaves.[18]

Carter's prosperity represented a pattern that had evolved throughout Brazos County between 1850 and 1860. Not only was there an increase in total population and in the number of slaves, but the amount of land in cultivation and the value of farms had mushroomed. The number of horses, mules, work oxen, and cattle also expanded; the increase was greatest in the number of cattle.[19] During this period of extremely rapid economic growth, the Houston and Texas Central Railroad, chartered in 1848, was extended to Millican in the southern limits of the county. The genesis of the City of Bryan, the county's most influential trading center, had been rooted in the anticipation that the railroad would continue northward through the county.

William Joel Bryan, a nephew of Stephen F. Austin, aided county development when he sold part of his land grant in the northern part of Brazos County as a right-of-way for the Houston and Texas Central. The townsite of Bryan was laid out in 1859 along the proposed railroad route. Surveyors set aside land for a courthouse, school, and Methodist church. The coming of the Civil War delayed construction of the railroad although the route already had been surveyed and graded as far as Hearne, some twenty miles north of Bryan. In 1860 Bryan sold his interests in town lots to Abram Groesbeeck and W. R. Baker, members of the board of directors of the Houston and Texas Central Railroad. With the end of the war, the town again boomed. County residents encouraged the growth by voting in October 1866 to move the county seat from Boonville to Bryan, a better location. The most effective stimulus, however, came when the railroad reached Bryan the following year.20

The moral atmosphere of Bryan was characteristic of a modern frontier town. Stores unabashedly stayed opened on Sunday. Numerous saloons encouraged drinking and gambling; on occasion shootings broke out. Business continued to prosper, and more proprietors were attracted to the area. The city was formally incorporated in 1872; city officials were appointed by the Republican dominated state legislature .21

The Civil War had had a devastating effect on the original investors in Brazos County. Many citizens lost much of their wealth with the freeing of slaves. Richard Carter's estate, valued at $44,000 before 1865, had plummeted to $9,800 by the close of the war. Although he had lost three-fourths of his fortune, he still remained in the county's upper economic bracket.22 In order to improve conditions and increase the money supply, businessmen knew they must attract new settlers into the region. Various enterprises were inaugurated. Promoters advertised land in foreign language papers, staged land giveaways, and provided temporary homes for new arrivals.23

Leaders took advantage also of a new interest in agriculture and engineering. The Bryan Male and Female Seminary had been established with the purpose of concentrating on those subjects. Harvey Mitchell organized the Central Texas Agricultural and Mechanical Association of Bryan in 1871 to sponsor annual fairs. The zeal behind these efforts to make the county more attractive economically culminated in a drive to secure the location of the state's first public institution of higher education near Bryan.24 Ironically, this effort also sparked the beginning of a rival community — College Station.

The Beginning of the College Community

Although a harrowing civil war monopolized the activities of the United States' government from 1860 to 1865, several remarkably progressive pieces of legislation, not directly related to the conflict, emerged from Congress. One such measure, the Morrill Land Grant Act of 1862, sought to make a utilitarian education, emphasizing agriculture and mechanical arts, accessible to the working class. The Act provided states with a permanent fund, derived from donated federal land, that would supply the financial means to start a college.

In 1866, Texas accepted 180,000 acres of federal land for the endowment of a land grant institution which was to be established within five years. Hampered by problems arising from Reconstruction, Texas officials delayed creating the school until the deadline set by Congress drew near. On April 17, 1871, the Agricultural and Mechanical College of Texas was officially established.[25] Governor Edmund Davis appointed three commissioners, John G. Bell, F. E. Grothaus, and George B. Slaughter, to select a suitable location for the college within thirty days. It was hoped, however much in vain, to construct the college buildings by July 1871 in order to comply with the terms of the agreement.[26]

The commissioners surveyed many sites, including ones in Austin, Galveston, Waco, San Marcos, Tehuacana, and Kellum Springs and Piedmont Springs in Grimes County. When the men visited Bryan, the citizens lavishly entertained them, tentatively promising to contribute $20,000 or $30,000 to the college. Although the commissioners were impressed, they would not commit themselves to the area. In fact, Commissioner Bell was eager to establish the college at Bellville in Austin County. On June 20, 1871, Harvey Mitchell met with the commission in Houston and on his own volition, donated 2,250 acres in an effort to guarantee the establishment of the institution near Bryan. The commissioners agreed to accept the contribution if they received title to the land within forty-eight hours. Otherwise, a site in Bellville would be selected.[27]

With the help of other Bryan citizens, Mitchell procured the necessary deeds and obtained money to purchase the needed land. Property of Harvey Mitchell, J. Frederick Cox, and Rebecca and Nelson Rector made up the 2,416-acre tract of land that was "granted, bargained, sold and released to A. and M. College" on June 21, 1871 in Houston. Brazos County later held a special election approving the sale of $22,000 in bonds to pay for the land appropriated to the college.[28]

The parcel of land designated for the new college was four miles south of Bryan. The institution was to be constructed on the highest summit of the region. An immense prairie, containing a scattering of post oak trees, enveloped the site; only thirty acres in the donated Rector section had ever been cultivated. The area had previously served as an assembly point for cattle drives, and a few wild mustangs and longhorns still roamed the open countryside. Other animal inhabitants included horned toads, scorpions, rabbits, deer, and wolves.[29]

Not all residents of Texas were satisfied with the site selected for the school. Some insinuated that the decision was shaded with intrigue, and claimed that the county's bid was the lowest one made. Others objected to the desolate environment. They argued that the "lands there about were among the poorest in the state, unfit for agriculture and that the region was very unhealthy."[30]

Although there were complaints about the surroundings and lack of salubrious climate, the location was not without its advantages. Brazos County in 1871 was near the center of the state's population. The college site was well drained, and the Houston and Texas Central Railroad ran through the center of the tract. The first architect for the college, Cale G. Forshey, was especially pleased with the site. He wrote:

The grounds I found adapted to the purpose almost as if designed by nature, or prescribed by a most skillful connoisseur. It would be difficult to find any other fault, except the want of water, and for this purpose we provide most amply by tanks or pools nearly to hand by nature; and by the cisterns already reported to you in the plans of the College building.[31]

Although the site of the state's first public institution of higher education had both its strengths and weaknesses, the decision to build had been made. The next step was to construct adequate campus facilities so that the instruction in agricultural and mechanical arts might proceed smoothly.

Work began on Old Main, the college's first building, in the fall of 1871. Unfortunately, progress ceased the following summer when the foundation and already erected walls were found to be faulty. After the hiring of a new architect and the letting of new contracts, the building was completed in January 1875.[32] The commission hoped to open the school in the fall of 1875, but neither student nor faculty housing had been assembled, and there was as yet no dining facility. In 1871, the legislature passed a measure requiring the college to provide suitable buildings to accommodate professors and their families; however, the legislators failed to appropriate funds for the homes or for a student "boarding hall" until 1875. With the completion of Steward Hall, later renamed Gathright Hall, and a few houses, the college was ready to open its doors to the students. That important event took place on October 4, 1876, with 106 students in attendance.[33] The event also signaled the beginning of a new community.

When persuading the commission to locate the college nearby, Bryan citizens had emphasized that the site was "far enough away from evil influences of the city so that the morals of the students would be protected."[34] Providing a wholesome environment for students was indeed important. Yet, the college's remoteness virtually precluded reliance on the established town for necessary amenities. An interesting turn of events had occurred. Bryan citizens, who had worked hard and contributed much money to insure the establishment of the college nearby, found that the distance between the town and the school encouraged the development of an independent community closer to the college.

The college community was defined by a cluster of campus buildings perched on top of the knoll, and a few structures assembled near the railroad track. On campus, Old Main and Steward Hall faced west, looking out toward the flagstop along the railroad. A block of five professors' homes stood to the southeast of the central buildings. These two-story brick homes, incorporating a common style of architecture, were placed one beside another thus encouraging the sobriquets, "Quality Row" and "The Line."[35]

A post office under the supervision of Henry Parsons stood near the railroad tracks. Letters sent to those on campus were addressed to "College Station, Texas." The U.S. Post Office Department had designated the community with that title in February 1877. Campus dwellers immediately began to refer to their community as College Station rather than Bryan. By April 1877 Thomas S. Gathright, the first president of Texas A. and M., along with the other residents began to cross out "Bryan" on the letterhead of the college stationery and insert "College Station."[36]

Although the post office designation suggested the existence of a town, off-campus community growth was minimal for at least fifty years. In the early years, the Texas A. and M. Board of Directors encouraged off-campus development. In June 1877, for example, the directors leased three acres of college land adjacent to the post office to Henry Parsons, granting him permission to open a general store provided that no intoxicating liquor would be sold on the premises. The board was especially eager for the construction of a lodging house for visitors near the railroad because guests had to be accommodated in rooms on campus. To anyone who would erect a "house of entertainment," the officials agreed to lease ten acres of college land west of the railroad.37 Five acres were leased to the second postmaster, Edward B. Pugh, but he never constructed the much-needed facilities.38

One building of permanence, the railroad depot, was constructed in 1883 when the Houston and Texas Central began making regular stops at College Station. That same year William C. Boyett, a long-time resident of the surrounding area, became the postmaster. He purchased the general store and was awarded a contract to furnish fresh meat to the college.39 Apparently, there were little or no additional developments in the off-campus area before the turn of the century. Because all of the citizens of the fledgling community lived on the campus, the college grew more rapidly than did the surrounding town. Off-campus housing and lodging facilities did not become available until the 1920s.

It was not an easy task for the college administrators to bring order to the untamed environment or to furnish necessary facilities for the campus community; nor did they accomplish these objectives overnight. For the first twenty-five years, the campus remained in an inchoate state. Robert Franklin Smith, a professor of mathematics, described the campus as a "wild waste" which was considered unsafe at night. In a brief memoir of the college's early days, Smith recounted an incident in which an unidentified wild animal peered into the dining room window one night. Thirty students and a few professors rushed out to kill the predator only to have it escape. "The howling of wolves," Smith recorded, "furnished an every night and all night serenade."40

The college did not have modern utilities until the late 1890s. For years, an antiquated sewer system served the inhabitants. Drinking water was collected in cisterns because well water was sulfurous and corrosive. Wood stoves heated the dormitories and homes.41 The college first received electricity in 1890, when the directors approved a contract with the Water, Ice, and Electric Company of Bryan. A joint investigative committee later suggested that the institution establish its own independent electric plant, and at the same time institute a curriculum for training in electrical engineering. The embryonic system went into operation in November 1893.42

In May 1899, the Texas legislature appropriated $104,000 for improvements on the A. and M. campus. The appropriation helped lift the college out of its rudimentary environment. Funds were allotted for such facilities and improvements as a steam heating plant, a sewage system, five new homes for professors, and a new electrical and ice plant.43 The new additions made the community more self-sufficient. The college was able to provide for the needs of a moderate size school population. That ability would lessen with the increased growth of the school.

Surrounding Rural Farm Communities

Efforts of Brazos residents to attract new inhabitants to the county bore fruit in the late 1870s and early 1880s. Immigrants from Southern and Eastern Europe migrated to the United States in large numbers during those years, and many made their way to the agricultural fields of Texas. Italians first arrived in Brazos County in the 1870s. An Italian steamship line maintained an agent in Bryan, and by the late 1880s, Brazos County had the largest colony of Italian farmers in the entire United States.44 Other immigrant families settling in the area were recent arrivals from Russia, Germany, Poland, Austria, and two European provinces, Bohemia and Moravia, which later were incorporated in Czechoslovakia.

To these agrarian-oriented immigrants, Brazos County represented an excellent environment for beginning a new life. Descriptions of the county, such as the one published in the South and Western Texas Guide for 1878, encouraged settlement. The guide reported that Brazos County, a part of the great cotton-producing region of Texas, enjoyed uniform temperatures and abundant rainfall. The fertile upland soil was easily cultivated, yielding a variety of crops including cereal grains, vegetables, and fruits. Promotional literature emphasized the excellence of bottom lands along the river courses. One pamphlet proclaimed that the "richness and fertility of Brazos bottoms have become famous and their productions are not excelled in any part of the world."[45] Most importantly, older residents, according to the guide, eagerly welcomed immigrants into their midst. Inspired by this and similar accounts, small communities, populated by native European farmers, germinated throughout the county in the late nineteenth century years.

One such settlement, the community of Shiloh, developed in close proximity to the Texas A. and M. College. Shiloh, located two miles south of the campus, consisted predominantly of Czech immigrants, but also included families native to Poland and Germany. Turmoil in Central Europe in the 1880s, accompanied by military oppression and religious persecutions, encouraged these people to leave their homelands.[46]

Frank Stasney, one of the early settlers in the Shiloh area, fled to America to escape the feudalistic system that shackled the peasants of Central Europe. In 1867 Stasney bought his first plot of land in Brazos County. In time, he would own approximately 550 acres extending west from Carter Creek to present-day Highway 6. Like Stasney, most families in the area purchased enough acreage so that their farms stretched two or three miles. Families

such as the Kapchinskies, Blazeks, Tureks, and Boriskies lived in the same vicinity as the Stasneys. The Sebestas, Bomnskies, Hrdlickas, and others settled closer to the Houston and Texas Central Railroad line. Immigrant farmers also purchased land surrounding the college. Some of the families who settled near the campus were the Taubers to the north, the Varas to the east, and the Holiks to the south.[47]

These encircling, fair-sized farms, populated by only a handful of people, perhaps served to intensify the isolated condition of the college.

The community of Shiloh, its name derived from religious origins, developed as did other communities scattered through the county. Rural families, living reasonably close, banded together in order to provide support for each other. The farmers generally were involved in similar agricultural pursuits. They planted crops for their own families and to sell to the college or to merchants in Bryan. Livestock, such as cattle, goats, hogs, and chickens, was raised for the farmer's own use; only a small amount was sold locally. The families, not always of the same nationality, strove for the same goals and were not hindered by ethnic differences. The children played together even when they did not speak the same language. Herman Krenek, the grandson of Frank Stasney, recounted such a situation from his childhood days. "We had Polish friends. [the] Kapchinskies would come in. The boy would talk to me in Polish. I would talk to him in Czech, and we would play all day long."[48]

Some residents supplemented their farming with other industrious enterprises. Stasney established a vineyard and a mill, and his family enjoyed homemade molasses and wine. He also constructed a blacksmith shop where he repaired his tools along with those of his neighbors. The farmers owned only the basic farming implements which dulled easily with continual use. Stasney spent much time sharpening sweeps, hoes, shovels, and other equipment.[49]

Farming with only these rudimentary instruments required tremendous effort on the part of the farmers. More efficient equipment was too expensive to be purchased by one individual. Six men of the Shiloh community, spurred by quandary, organized and chartered the Czechoslovakian Agricultural and Good Will Club in 1881. The organization, its name first delineated in the Czechoslovakian language, became known as the Shiloh Club. The original members pooled their money and bought such modern equipment as a plow, a walking cultivator, and planters. The tools belonged to the club, but they were available for use by any member. Those joining the organization paid a S1.20 membership fee and ten cents a month dues.[50] Over time the club evolved from an agriculturally-oriented organization into a socially-oriented one. The Shiloh Club is in existence today.

Rural living conditions remain primitive for many years. Electricity was not furnished to the Shiloh area until the 1930s; wood stoves and kerosene lamps served as the source of heat and light. Septic tanks also were not installed until the 1930s; outhouses functioned as the only bathroom facility. Children carried well water to the house in buckets several times a day. During the summer the stifling heat forced families to sleep on the porch which earlier had been splashed with water. "It was tough," explain Herman Krenek, "It wasn't easy, but you didn't know anything better."[51]

The preservation of food also presented a problem. Some of the harvest could be canned and placed in a cool cellar. Food used during the week, however, could be kept from perishing only if protected by ice. Farmers dug a hole in the ground, placed a block of ice with the produce in the hole,

and covered the opening with a cloth. A 100-pound block of ice bought in Bryan on Saturday would last until the following Thursday.[52]

In the autumn hogs were butchered so that meat would be available for the evening meals through wintertime. During the summer months, preservation of meat was not possible. One family could not consume all the meat of a slaughtered animal before it became rancid. In order to prevent waste, twelve Shiloh families formed a meat club. Each week a family would kill a beef, divide it into twelve parts, and distribute it among the members. A family received around twelve pounds, which usually lasted three days.[53]

Each week the farmers in Shiloh traveled into Bryan to sell their crops and buy essential commodities. The family members packed their wagon in the early morning hours and began their trek along a dirt and gravel path into the county's major town, passing Texas A. and M. College on their way. Bryan, in the late 1880s, had become a manufacturing and trading center. Stores lined the main streets, and the saloons, located on each block, provided refreshments and entertainment.[54] A grist mill, a cottonseed mill, and two planing mills were in operation as well as a chair factory, a carriage and wagon factory, and a cotton gin. Cotton buyers from larger cities were on hand seasonally. By the end of the nineteenth century, buyers shipped 20,000 bales from Bryan to Galveston annually.[55] After selling their produce and buying weekly supplies, families headed back home and reached their homestead by twilight.[56]

Many of the farmers in Shiloh sold vegetables, fruits, and livestock to families on campus. Some had regular customers, and delivered eggs and butter each week. Frank Stasney sold much of his harvest to Bernard Sbisa, the manager for many years of dining facilities on the campus. As a child, Herman Krenek accompanied his grandfather to the college where Stasney displayed for Sbisa a cornucopia of crops — corn, peanuts, cantaloupes, watermelon, peaches, pears, or whatever else was in season. Stasney also provided Sbisa with some poultry including squabs or baby pigeons. Since they were considered a delicacy, Krenek felt certain that only the professors were served the squabs.[57]

By the turn of the century, a few commercial establishments were in operation in Shiloh. In 1911 Krenek's father built a grocery store that remained in business until the 1930s. The Golden Rule Poultry Farm was established with the purpose of raising and selling chickens on a commercial scale. Once a month and on holidays, local people held dances at Shiloh Hall, bringing in orchestras from Bryan. Shiloh Hall remained at the same location until 1975, when it was moved to the northern border of the county.[58]

The children of Shiloh attended a county school that was located at the present intersection of Highway 6 and Farm to Market (FM) Road 2818. A two room building served forty to fifty students; one room contained the first through the sixth grades, and the other held the seventh and eighth grades. The children walked to school, carrying their shoes if it rained. School was in session on the average of five months a year because the money allotted for operations lasted only that long. In 1920, the newly-formed A. and M. Consolidated School District absorbed the county school.[59]

Although the community no longer remains, four acres in College Station's cemetery connects Shiloh's past to the city today. Mrs. William G. Rector deeded four acres to the Methodist Church in 1870 to be used as a cemetery for settlers at Shiloh. The Shiloh Club assumed the responsibility for keeping up the grounds. When College Station acquired those few acres and the surrounding land for a city cemetery, the Shiloh Club continued to donate money for the care of the original cemetery.[60] The community of Shiloh eventually disappeared; its lands were absorbed by the city. The heritage of the immigrants, however, does remain. It is incorporated into the many facets of the city's character.

Further Development of the Campus Community

At the turn of the century, Texas A. and M. was gaining recognition and stature as a leading educational institution. The college curriculum emphasized theoretical study as well as practical application. For those students enrolled in mechanical arts, machine shops and equipment provided essential practical experience; those in agricultural studies were introduced to field work and the handling of animals.[61]

Growth in student population placed demands on the school that were difficult to satisfy. Texas A. and M. was still very much isolated, engulfed in a sea of prairie and farmland. The campus itself was barren; only a few trees stood among the buildings. The sole evidence of landscaping on the college was the line of cedar trees that bordered the road leading from Old Main to the railroad station. The roads and sidewalks on campus were primitive. Sidewalks, blanketed with a thin layer of cinder and gravel, became, as one resident observed, "small rivulets during the rainy weather."[62]

One of the constant concerns for college officials in the new century was the furnishing of housing for students and faculty and guest accommodations for visitors. As early as 1906, tents served as quarters for some students and were in continual use until after World War I.[63] The school constructed several more cottages for faculty south of the drill field and also near the peach orchard on the north side of campus.64 Rooms for visitors were non-existent. To alleviate this problem, a few faculty members organized the A. and M. College Club and proceeded to build The Shirley, a two-story frame building, the first hotel on campus.65

A committee appointed by A. and M.'s Board of Directors met with citizens of Bryan to encourage them to provide housing for college employees. The committee even suggested that Bryan citizens develop a residential and commercial area near the college. To facilitate development, the board requested that W. C. Boyett place some of his property at the north end of the campus on the market "so that there may be built adjacent to the college a community which would relieve the congested conditions on campus." When no development occurred by 1912, the directors set aside land on the northern side of campus so that businesses could be established. Eventually a butcher shop, shoe repair, tailor, barber, and photo gallery offered their services to residents on campus. Boyett was given a five-year lease to continue his "first class grocery store" on college grounds.66 College residents obtained access to facilities in Bryan only with the completion of a trolley line which provided a reliable mode of transportation between the two communities.

The ability to furnish an adequate transportation system between Bryan and the college remained at an impasse for nearly thirty-five years. Houston and Texas Central train took college residents into Bryan, but scheduling allowed little time to take care of business. Travelers in horse-drawn buggies or those on foot could use a sand and gravel road that paralleled the railroad tracks and eventually veered east to connect with Bryan's main street. The path, however, was dusty and rutted, and pedestrians had right-of-way over wagons.67 In 1897 faculty members organized a bicycle club, and the college financed the construction of a bicycle path adjacent to the railroad tracks. Professors and their wives cycled between College Station and Bryan along the trail for three years, but maintenance of the path became increasingly difficult, and the club ceased to function in 1900.68

Different presidents of the college promoted the development of an effective transportation system. David Franklin Houston, president of Texas A. and M. between 1902 and 1905, addressed the Business League of Bryan on September 1904 and suggested the construction of an interurban railway linking Bryan to the college.69 No action was taken until 1908 when O. E. Gammill, a businessman from Shreveport, Louisiana, agreed to finance the construction of a gasoline-powered interurban railway. By June 1910 the line was making scheduled runs on the hour between Bryan and College Station.70

Nicknamed the "Toonerville Trolley," the Bryan-College Interurban transported passengers with two cars that could be coupled with special park trailers. The fare was ten cents for a single trip or fifteen cents for a round trip; ticket books, containing passes for fifty rides, were available for five dollars. The slogan "To College the Easy Way" advertised the new transportation system, but the ride was not always smooth or without complications. Casey Jones, the motorman, attempted to run the street cars on schedule, but occasionally the failure of the trolley to start or its proclivity to jump the track prevented adherence to the posted schedule. The trolley had trouble climbing hills. At Hillcrest, a long incline north of the college, passengers helped push the trolley up the slope. Electric trolley cars, installed in 1915, had more power and carrying capacity.71 The Interurban operated until 1927, when the Bryan Traction Company replaced the railway with buses.

Although Bryan was accessible by the thirty-minute trolley ride, persons connected with the college tended to remain on or near the campus. Since the college community was still of a modest size, social life on campus was pleasant. Card parties and dances were held in faculty homes. Picnics were popular during the summer, the "Fish Tank" being the favorite picnic spot. The Fish Tank, a swimming hole fed by springs, was located three miles from campus near present Easterwood Airport. Young couples rode out to the picnic area in hay wagons or traveled in buggies. The highlight of the outing was the consumption of refreshing watermelons which had been cooling under wet burlap sacks during the day.[72]

Other programs on campus accommodated the residents' religious and cultural interests. The chapel offered worship services on Sunday and devotional hours during the week. A Lyceum brought to campus lecturers, male quartets, and magicians. The wide veranda of the Old Mess Hall provided a lovely setting for student dances.[73] The college even operated a zoo. Located on the west side of the railroad tracks, the zoo housed lions, tigers, snakes, ostriches, an elephant, and a menagerie of native American animals.[74] By the 1920s college residents were well supplied with entertainment and felt less isolated. There was a need, however, desired by both the officials of the institution and residents, for privately-owned homes off campus grounds.

The First Off-Campus Residential Subdivisions

The number of faculty homes had grown to seventy-five by 1925, and yet, there still was not enough housing for all the faculty families. The task of apportioning available housing to the faculty was troublesome, and younger members of the staff felt that the assignments were inequitable. Faculty members without enough tenure to receive campus housing had to look for accommodations in Bryan.[75] The less-desirable housing was smaller, older cottages scattered along the fringes of the campus. These dwellings were constructed of wood and hastily assembled. Ernest Langford recalled that his first home at Texas A. and M. was the "sorriest, most dilapidated house on campus."[76] Although he was later assigned a better home, Langford built his own residence in the College Park addition at the first opportunity. Professors as well as college officials were encouraged when College Park, the first residential area adjacent to the campus, opened.

College Park, located south of the college's border, was launched by Southside Development Company under the auspices of Dr. Floyd B. Clark. Dr. Clark, professor of economics, along with four other professors incorporated the company on August 4, 1921. Clark had the assurance of Dr. William B. Bizzell, president of Texas A. and M., that when ten residences were erected in the new subdivision, college utility lines would be extended to the end of A. and M.'s property where they could be connected to the privately-owned transmission lines. The development company bought sixty-six acres south of the campus from Ed Hrdlicka in 1921 and seventeen additional acres in 1923. Professors were hired to work in their off-hours to aid in the development of College Park. Frederick W. Hensel, professor of landscape architecture, supervised the planting of the area and constructed a small lake in the center of the subdivision.[77]

The lots in College Park essentially sold themselves; a salesman was never hired. Southside Development Company's leaders stipulated that lots could not be sold for speculative purposes, and they reserved the rights to buy back the land parcels if no construction on the property had occurred within three years. The company never lost money, and there were no foreclosures.78

Hershel Burgess, a former student at Texas A. and M., bought eighty acres of land next to College Park and formed the Oakwood Realty Company in 1932. He subdivided the property and created Oakwood addition. Burgess was able to take advantage of assistance offered by the Federal Housing Administration (FHA) which stimulated homebuilding in the residential areas off campus. "It [the FHA-approved loan] made it easy," Burgess explained, "for professors and other A. and M. employees to buy their own homes, and they just filled up my little addition down there pretty quickly." According to Burgess, Oakwood was the first FHA-approved project between Houston and Dallas.79

More residents were moving off the campus, and yet, a municipal government did not exist to supply essential services. The burden of providing amenities fell to the developer of the subdivision. Burgess, for example, erected poles and electric lines from Oakwood to the A. and M. campus. The realty company laid water pipes which were tied into the college's water system. Residents had to install their own septic tanks. In order to pay for utility use, street upkeep, and garbage pick-up, Oakwood Realty taxed the residents according to the size of their lots.80 The streets were poorly constructed, but they allowed access to the area. To dispose of the subdivision's garbage, Burgess hired "Mayor" Wash Findley from Wellborn. Burgess recalled vividly garbage day in the neighborhood:

This old black man, Wash Findley, had a wagon and mule and it was his job to pick up the garbage ... [Findley] had about three or four kids. The oldest one was eleven or twelve and then on down. They would always stack the garbage in the wagon. The little white kids would follow them around.

Findley had two or three dogs that he lashed onto the wagon with a string or something, and it was kind of a comedy to see them coming ... the kids following, hollering, and carrying on. Findley did that for several years. When the city organized, then the city took over [the garbage pickup]. That was real country — real backward way of doing it, but that was all, we could do in those days.81

The realty companies such as Southside and Oakwood attempted to provide for the needs of the residents but, within a few years, it was apparent that a true governmental organization had become essential. A community had existed for sixty years, and an off-campus residential area had been developing since the 1920s. At the end of the 1930s, a group of college professors gathered together to create a town that would better fulfill the needs of their community.

Chapter II

Incorporating and organizing college station, 1936 - 1942

OFF-CAMPUS RESIDENTS occasionally discussed the merits of organizing a local government, but they did not succeed in establishing a city until the late 1930s. The leadership that college officials had provided the community since its inception perhaps lessened the urgency to create a separate governmental entity. Yet, increased growth of the college and the off-campus residential and business areas during the 1930s magnified the need for municipal incorporation. From 1936 to 1942, residents concentrated on bringing the City of College Station into existence and. establishing basic city functions. In these early years, the city remained strongly attached to the college. Professors were leaders in the community, campus activities were discussed in city meetings, and the city relied on many campus facilities. Nonetheless, incorporation marked the true beginning of the municipality of College Station.

During the 1930s ever greater numbers of students, faculty members, and businessmen gravitated toward the college community. The initial residential areas expanded, and a new addition, College Hills Estates, developed at the East Gate. A small business district flourished along the northern fringe of the campus. When the Post Office and Boyett's Store were relocated at North Gate in the early twenties, other businesses, to the satisfaction of college officials, also settled in the area. Immediately prior to incorporation, various merchants served the college population. Students frequented the barbershops, cleaners, military supply outlets, and tailors. Residents could purchase medical supplies at Aggieland Pharmacy or Lipscomb's Pharmacy and groceries at Luke's Camp Grocery or Charlie's Food Market. Occasionally, families enjoyed a meal out at The College Inn or at the Texas A. and M. Grill.[1]

One major reason for off-campus expansion in the 1930s was the corresponding growth of Texas A. and M. College. The college entered a transitional period which propelled the institution forward from its formative past. In July 1931, Texas A. and M. deeded approximately eight acres along its eastern campus boundary to the State Highway Department to facilitate the construction of State Highway 6 from Navasota to Waco.[2] With the completion of Texas 6 in 1936, the once isolated institution and its community became more accessible to prospective students and residents.

The school experienced spectacular growth in several areas. From 1934 to 1938 enrollment increased from 3,000 to 6,000.[3] The Agricultural Experiment Station and the Extension Service underwent expansion, and agencies, such as the Texas Forest Service and the Triple A, established headquarters on campus.[4] These developments mandated the construction of additional campus facilities.

The enlarged building program launched to meet these demands changed the orientation of the campus. The construction of an administration building that faced the new highway signaled the relocation of the main entrance from west to east. New dormitories and a dining hall were built in the southern portion of campus, a fair distance from the center of college activities. The location of existing faculty homes had prevented the construction of new structures adjacent to older, longest established facilities.[5]

College officials became concerned when residential housing blocked expansion in the logic areas of the campus. During the 1930s the Board of Directors frequently discussed the possibility of requiring faculty members to move off-campus and of tearing down or removing faculty homes. Providing faculty housing had become an exhaustive burden, no longer necessary because residential developments off-campus existed to accommodate faculty families. In September 1939, the directors ordered professors to move off-campus. They were given until September 1, 1941 to find new residences.[6] It had never been intended that Texas A. and M. should function as landlord for the academic population.

Residents soon considered the possibility of creating their own municipal government. A city government could oversee the installation and maintenance of utilities, the extension and repair of streets, and the regulation of growth. A police and a fire department were needed desperately. Of course, inhabitants of the college community did have the option of asking Bryan to annex them. Bryan, with a population of more than 7,000, had the ability to provide basic city services.[7] Some people did decide that it would be advantageous to be part of an established community. Residents of the North Oakwood subdivision, located north of the campus along Highway 6, unanimously voted to be annexed. Most people, however, were not eager to be a part of Bryan, and there was some feeling that Bryan had hindered the development of the off-campus area.[8]

By the mid-1930s, a community with unique characteristics had grown up around the college. Members of this homogeneous community felt close to their neighbors, understood their needs, and knew best how to solve communal problems. With incorporation, the community which had begun many years earlier would at last have legality. Incorporation would "insure retention of College Station, Texas for all time to come."[9]

Incorporation

The first concrete step toward incorporation occurred on March 4, 1938, when twenty-three men, representing various interests on campus and in the off-campus community, appeared before the Board of Directors of Texas A. and M. College. This self-organized committee requested a statement of policy by the board on the question of incorporation. The group presented a list of twelve "good and salient reasons for incorporation of the City of College, Texas." This was the only occasion when anyone referred to the future town simply as "College, Texas."[10]

The petitioners gave assurance that the proposed city government would concentrate on meeting the needs of the community and would not interfere with the administration of the college. The status of college-owned utility and distribution lines, for example, would remain un-changed, and would not be subjected to any franchise, tax, or regulation.[11]

The petition enumerated benefits that incorporation would provide. Public health and sanitation would be improved by the construction of sewage disposal facilities, by the provision of garbage collection at the North Gate business district and residential areas, and by the establishment of health standards for commercial businesses. Traffic and transportation problems could be eased. A municipal corporation could regulate traffic in the congested off-campus areas, grant franchises to bus lines and taxi companies, and provide a street building and repair program.[12]

A local government could also address such issues as fire safety and police protection. Standard codes for buildings, wiring, and electrical equipment could be enforced and thus prevent the construction of firetraps. The existence of a fire department would result in a reduction in fire insurance rates by as much as fifty percent. Police protection would also be a deterrent to crime.[13]

Finally, the proposal stressed the need for a municipal government to sustain the A. and M. Consolidated School District which had been established on campus in the early 1920s. The petitioners wrote, "Incorporation is the only salvation for the public schools in this Independent School District, and this problem alone makes the proposal worthwhile even should all other reasons be ruled out."[14] It was believed that if a city government was not organized, the school system would lose taxable land to other school districts and revert back to the jurisdiction of the county. The loss would be tragic for the children of the community. The petition concluded by reiterating that the residents desired to incorporate their own town in order to solve problems that had arisen in their community.

The Board of Directors immediately responded, assuring the petitioners that the board had no objections to incorporation, and they advised the citizens to include a belt of land around the campus in their proposed city. The incorporators called a community meeting for March 22, 1938, so that all concerned parties might debate the merits of incorporation and so that an incorporation committee could be selected if citizens so desired. John Thomas Lamar McNew, a professor of highway engineering and leader of the delegation that had appeared before the Board of Directors chaired the meeting.[15]

One result of the meeting was the election of ten men to an incorporation committee, consisting of two representatives from each of the five sections of the community. Subsequently, John Henry Binney, a professor of mathematics, headed the group. The primary function of the committee was to circulate a petition for incorporation and then submit to the county judge the petition with at least fifty signatures along with a description and a map of the area to be incorporated. According to the Revised Civil Statutes of the State of Texas, the county judge would establish a date for a vote on incorporation![16]

Between March and June of 1938, the committee collected more than 165 signatures. According to the proposed plat of the new town, College Station would include the Texas A. and M. campus, the College Park and Oakwood additions, the western boundaries of the Southern Pacific Railroad properties, the business district at North Gate, and part of the College Hills Estates addition along Highway 6.[17] The petition reached Brazos County Judge John Marion Ferguson on June 2, and he set October 19, 1938, as the election date.[18]

Apparently, while citizens of the college community worked to incorporate their own town, Bryan officials looked into the possibility of annexing that same area. Early residents recall that Mayor E. E. Yeager and Attorney Law Henderson of Bryan favored annexation to the older community.[19] Because Texas statutes limit the amount of land a city can incorporate in a single year, Bryan was unable to annex the academic community. Bryan officials did, however, annex as much land as legally possible. The new city limits of Bryan extended almost to the North Gate business district, and encompassed areas that previously had been part of the A. and M. Consolidated School District. This annexation severely limited future northern expansion of the proposed city and siphoned off part of its school district.[20] The old rivalry between the two communities, which had become dormant, was renewed and continued to increase in intensity over this issue.

On October 19, 1938, citizens voted 217 to 39 to incorporate the City of College Station, a community which had existed for more than sixty years.[21] The designated polling place, the Southern Pacific depot, added a symbolic touch to the election since the city derived its name from that of the railroad station.

Since the new city had fewer than 5,000 inhabitants, it was required to operate under guidelines established in Title 28 of the 1925 Revised Civil Statutes. The citizens were to elect a mayor, five aldermen, and a city marshal. In order to insure one definite ticket of city officers, the incorporation committee called a mass meeting for November 11 to be held in the Chemistry Lecture Room on campus.[22] At the meeting the residents nominated John H. Binney for mayor and Letcher P. Gabbard for alderman at large. The assembly then broke into groups that corresponded with their place of residence to select a representative from their area Gilbert J. Samuelson, George W. Wilcox, Alva Mitchell, and Luther G. Jones filled the remaining positions of aldermen, and John S. Hopper received a nomination as city marshal.[23] Each of these men, with one exception, took office on November 28, 1938; Ernest Langford replaced Mr. Samuelson. All the original city officers were faculty members of Texas A. and M. College.[24]

Almost immediately the new city faced a serious problem when the comptroller of the college questioned whether the Texas Constitution allowed employees of the state to receive state warrants while serving as city officials. Sections 33 and 40 of Article 16 of the Texas Constitution prohibited payment of warrants to a person who held two positions of public trust. In December 1938, an assistant to Attorney General William McCraw unofficially ruled that the recently elected officials could not serve in both capacities and receive payment from the state. Each of the men decided to forego taking the oath of office or starting municipal operation until the city could seek a formal opinion from Attorney-General elect Gerald Mann at the first of the year.[25]

City officers and residents were dismayed by these complications since all had worked hard to establish the city government. Ernest Langford recalled, "We had five councilmen and nothing to do but twiddle our thumbs. We'd meet over a cup of coffee and talk."[26] To the citizens' delight, Attorney General Mann ruled on February 24, 1939, that college professors were not considered state officers, and thus College Station's city officials could draw state pay. The officers were sworn into office, and College Station began functioning as a municipality that same day.[27] Ironically, a similar issue would reappear in the early 1970s and again create turmoil for the city.

The First City Government Begins Operation

On February 25, 1939, College Station City Council held its first council meeting in the Administration Building on campus. After a brief discussion, the council posed for a group picture which appeared in the *Battalion*, *Bryan Eagle*, and various newspapers of neighboring cities. During the first week of the city's existence, the council received a letter from the Bryan mayor and city commission which expressed good wishes and offered cooperation. Bryan officials agreed to attend a future council meeting to discuss matters pertinent to both cities.[28]

City officials decided to meet once a week in Room 400 of the Agricultural Building until the operation of the city was smoothly under way. The first few meetings were devoted to working out administrative details. Joseph A. Orr, professor of civil engineering and a future council member, agreed to stake out the boundaries of College Station. The council appointed a city attorney, city engineer, sanitary engineer, and city health officer. Sidney Loveless, a recent graduate of Texas A. and M., was designated city secretary; his regular duties were combined with those of treasurer and city assessor and collector. Loveless, who received a small salary, held office hours Thursday through Saturday to conduct city business.[29]

The young municipality soon faced another election, the annual election of officers in April for all general law cities. The mayor and the aldermen decided to seek second terms. On April 4, 1939, voters re-elected John Binney as mayor and Luther Jones, Letcher Gabbard, and George Wilcox as aldermen. Ernest Langford and Alva Mitchell, however, were replaced in their positions by Samuel A. Lipscomb and Wayne E. Long. In order to establish alternating terms for aldermen as specified in the Civil Statues, the men drew lots. Jones and Gabbard drew one year terms; Lipscomb, Long, and Wilcox, two year terms.[30]

Instead of continuing to rely on campus space, College Station officials decided to establish their own office, one which would be used solely for council meetings and city business. Joe Sosolik had an available room over his Aggieland Studio at North Gate which rented for $17.50 per month with utilities furnished. The council agreed to the terms and met for the first time in the new quarters on May 18, 1939.[31]

Since the city leaders budgeted $4,320 for expenses in 1939, it became necessary to set up a tax program. The council set a tax rate of $.60 on each $100.00 of real or personal property and required citizens to submit an inventory of their property by July 15, 1939. Three commissioners served as a Board of Equalization to examine the assessments, and taxes became due on December 15.[32] In order to meet immediate obligations, the council authorized Binney and Loveless to borrow on behalf of the city until the end of the year.[33] The First State Bank and Trust Company of Bryan was declared the official depository of College Station.[34]

The council was encouraged when the residents approved the tax renditions. Impressed by the community spirit, the council, in an article in the *Battalion*, thanked the residents for their support.

When the residents of a locality band themselves together and resolve to make of theirs a better community in which to live, and accept the burden of financing the movements to make it such, then progress is being made. It is felt by the board of aldermen that such is the case here at College Station. By working together and cooperating with each other, this city can become a model after which others can pattern themselves.[35]

Officials quickly realized that College Station required a stronger financial foundation before the city could provide customary municipal services. The aldermen hoped to utilize many of the facilities offered on campus and thus met periodically with the A. and M.'s Board of Directors during the city's first year. The directors accommodated the young city in many ways. The college sanitary engineer and his deputies collected the garbage in College Station. The directors authorized the city's use of the college fire department on a fee basis. College sergeants worked as deputy city marshals, and students served on temporary traffic duty.[36]

From the outset, the council encouraged A. and M. students to participate in city government. When the *Battalion*, the college newspaper, was adopted as the city's official newspaper, the 1939-1940 editor, Bill Murray, appeared before the council to offer cooperation in running items about the city. He also suggested that the council discuss the concerns of the student body with cadets. City officials found merit in the proposal and invited a student from the Student Welfare Committee and a representative from the *Battalion* to sit in on council meetings.[37]

One of the first goals set by officials was the acquisition of all utility distribution systems and the right to manage utility services. Developers were eager to shift responsibility to municipal authority, and residents desired a consistent, city-wide operation of utility services. Without greater financial resources than the city could master, it could not purchase the existing systems outright, and therefore, had to obtain them in a piecemeal fashion.

The city acquired its first utility lines in late 1939 when residents from the Boyett addition in the north area of town appeared before the council to urge the city to take over the power, sewer, and water lines in their small subdivision.[38] After consultation with college officials, the council agreed to take jurisdiction over electric lines only.[39]

In February 1940, the council purchased facilities in the residential areas at Southside. The city paid $8,500 to Oakwood Realty Company and $15,000 to Southside Development Company for their electric, water, and sewer systems.[40] An inventory of the newly acquired equipment included such items as electric meters, poles and lines, transformers, water and sewer mains, laterals, outfall lines, fire plugs, and the sewer disposal system.[41]

By the end of the year, the city also bought the water lines in the Boyett addition and facilities in the recently developed West Park subdivision at Southside. The council also procured water and sewer utilities from College Hills Estates for $1,100.[42] The electric lines in College Hills were Rural Electricification Administration (REA) lines owned by Bryan, and to the chagrin of College Station officials, the city was not able to obtain the lines for several years.

College Station owned all the existing utility distribution systems within its limit by the end of 1940 except for the REA lines in College Hills. The city contracted with both Texas A. and M. and Bryan for utility services in the early days and would continue to do so until recent years. The City of College Station was on its feet. Luther Jones, one of the original councilmen, felt that College Station had become a true municipality once the city owned its distribution systems and managed its utility services. Growth, he recalled, was constant. "We [the council] always got pleasure in every new house that was built. It was surprising how fast people flocked in and built homes. Fortunately, we had a very ideal community, and everybody worked for the same purpose."[43]

The A. and M. Consolidated School District

Residents of College Station were determined that A. and M. Consolidated School District, the public school system which had originated on campus, would continue to serve the children of their community. The school district had recently encountered difficulties. It lost taxable land to Bryan, and it, too, was asked to vacate campus property. Although faced with the necessity of procuring land for a school and constructing educational facilities, the citizens were fervent about supporting their school district; it had provided education for their children since 1920.

The genesis of the school district began at some time around the first of the century. The Texas Legislature, in order to provide for the educational needs of the children of faculty at Texas A. and M., created the A. and M. College Independent School District on March I 0, 1909.[44] Since the district borders were the same as those of the college, the district included 3500 acres of land and buildings valued at $3,500,000. A school, however, did not immediately materialize. College land was state owned and thus not taxable. Campus families, with a total of only thirty to forty children, could not themselves support a modem school.[45] Instead, professors operated an informal tutoring service for the children.[46]

Under the provisions of the 1917 Smith-Hughes Act, funds were made available to Texas A. and M. for preparation of prospective agricultural teachers. The act stipulated, however, that students were to gain practical teaching experience in public schools. In order to meet the criteria of the agricultural teaching program and at the same time furnish an education for campus children, President William Bizzell and Professor Martin L. Hayes, head of the Department of Vocational Teaching, decided to establish a school on campus.[47]

Two major obstacles prevented implementation of their plan — obtaining adequate finances and gathering a sufficient number of students. Professor Hayes persuaded the State Board of Education to grant rural aid funds to finance the operation of the school. For the construction of a school building, President Bizzell made available $25,000 which previously had been appropriated by the legislature for a new president's home. In order to insure enough students, Hayes conceived of the idea to consolidate the school with common schools that were in close proximity to the campus. The rural districts of Rock Prairie, Union Hill, and Wellborn agreed to help launch the new school if transportation for their students could be provided.[48]

The new school, which was to be "a model of its kind," opened on September 28, 1920, with 160 students in attendance. The students met in Guion Hall for the first few weeks until the new building could be completed. When the classes moved into the new building, they found themselves without adequate supplies. The principal had to borrow surplus equipment from various departments on campus.[49] The high school curriculum was geared toward both college preparation and vocational studies. Ex-tracurricular activities such as athletics and a dramatic club were available. The first class, consisting of six students, graduated from A. and M. Consolidated in May, 1922.[50]

The young school district, inaugurated with sanguine aspirations, soon experienced problems. The school lost its first leaders; Professor Hayes died in the early twenties and Dr. Bizzell moved to Oklahoma in 1925. The college discontinued its teacher training program, and the legislature eliminated funds which previously had been appropriated for educational purposes. The school rapidly outgrew its only building, and the entire high school department had to be transferred to Pfeiffer Hall where it remained until it was moved off-campus. Expenses increased, but revenue from rural aid grants and local taxes failed to keep pace. In 1928 the four school districts consolidated and elected a board of seven trustees. Although financial burdens did not abate, the school managed to provide quality education through the 1930's.51

Toward the latter 1930s, the trustees sought to relieve the school's congested condition. In November 1938 a committee conferred with college officials to investigate the prospect for obtaining a new school site. The officials replied that they could not provide assistance, and thus implied that the school would eventually have to vacate the campus.52 The directors reasoned that the school district more appropriately belonged under the auspices of the newly-established municipality rather than the college.

At this same time, Bryan city commissioners and members of the Bryan school board offered to incorporate A. and M. Consolidated in their school district. Representatives from both school districts met in late 1938 to discuss the possibilities. Considering the financial situation of the consolidated school district, the proposal merited serious consideration. The *Bryan Eagle*, reported that even if the impending incorporation of the College Station community came to fruition, the two school districts, in all likelihood, would merge.53

College Station citizens, however, did not want their school district to be under the jurisdiction of another community. They petitioned the school board to hold a bond election which, if passed, would finance the construction of adequate facilities off-campus. On February 25, 1939 voters overwhelmingly approved the issuance of $75,000 in bonds for this project.54 In order to sell the bonds, the equalization board had to double the evaluation of all city property. Residents accepted the assessment without complaint.55

The school board hired Ernest Langford and Clarence Jack Finney, professors in the Architecture Department, to design the new facilities. Two school sites were under consideration, a fifteen acre tract in College Hills Estates and the Holik. Property site, also

of fifteen acres. Residents favored the Holik site. In order to purchase the land, some of the people organized a drive for funds and collected a total of $5,500.58 from 116 patrons.56 At the school board's April meeting, men favoring the Holik. Site explained its advantages. It was conveniently located and was situated adjacent to the land that the board had hoped to receive from the college. The site afforded access to facilities on campus such as the library, laboratories, and shops. Utilities were available from the Oakwood addition, and school patrons were willing to pay for connecting the school's lines to Oakwood. The board accepted this generous offer.57

Langford and Finney assigned their students the task of making the necessary surveys and designing the school; the architects, however, had final approval.58 The finished facilities consisted of four elementary units containing fourteen classrooms and additional office space, a high school with eight classrooms, and a building to house the industrial arts and music departments.59 Men from the community brought trees and shrubbery from the Brazos and Navasota river bottoms for transplanting at the new school site.60 The buildings were formally accepted on March 8, 1940.

Within a year, another bond election was approved to finance the construction of a gymnasium-auditorium building and an athletic field complete with a stadium.61 With the continuing support of the community, A. and M. Consolidated School District successfully made the transition from the jurisdiction of the college to that of the municipality.

Planning for Community Growth

Three distinct divisions of the city, present even in the pre-incorporated community, expanded during the 1940s. Each section had its own residential areas with accompanying shops. Since modes of transportation were limited in the early days, residents patronized neighborhood stores. North Gate continued to serve as the main business district. New additions to that area included a theatre, hardware store, dentist office, and a Methodist church.[62] Luke's Campus Grocery moved to East Gate where College Hills Estates continued to expand. New subdivisions were being added at Southside along with a small commercial development.[63]

One somewhat extravagant newspaper account described College Station as "the fastest growing city in Texas."[64] Community leaders and citizens were aware that they were in a position to institute programs at the outset that would insure orderly growth. In those initial years, the council established policies and organized committees to guide municipal expansion. Although these instruments of regulation were not utilized consistently until the late 1960s, the principle of directing growth was established at the city's inception.

According to one early developer, College Station became the first city between Houston and Dallas to establish zoning regulations.[65] Residents enthusiastically supported zoning because they believed it prevented loss in land values and eliminated "internal strife among the citizenship.[66] The city council created a Zoning Commission in July 1939 whose purpose was to recommend a comprehensive plan consisting of zoning districts and regulations which would make districting effective.[67] The city's first zoning ordinance went into operation in January 1949.[68] To complement the Zoning Commission, Mayor Binney appointed a City Planning Board in November 1939. At the request of Texas Governor W. Lee O'Daniel, the board also functioned as an Industrial Development Committee.[69]

The first city council made provisions for the creation of the City Parks Board.

Beginning in May 1939, the Parks Board had authority to manage parks and public grounds for recreational and beautification purposes. Although there was no official city park, the board had authority to receive grants of money and donations of labor and materials.[70]

The young municipality had undertaken many projects and had made substantial progress during its first year of existence. Unfortunately, it soon lost the sagacious leadership of its first mayor. In early 1940 John Binney was involved in a serious car accident. The injuries he sustained in the accident prevented him from fulfilling his mayoral term. The council accepted Binney's resignation effective April 1940, and a new election to select a mayor and two aldermen was slated for the same month.[71]

A group of concerned citizens met to discuss who might make a suitable replacement for Binney. The fledging community wanted a strong leader at its helm. Consequently, the committee decided to ask Colonel Frank G. Anderson, the track coach at. Texas A. and M., to run for mayor. Anderson had many stalwart qualities and was not afraid to work for what he believed.[72]

Anderson, born in Sparta, Tennessee in 1891, came to Texas A. and M. in the early 1920s. Dana X. Bible, then A. and M.'s football coach, had been Anderson's high school teacher and college coach, and he encouraged his former student to come to Texas. Anderson became the track coach at Texas A. and M. in 1922 and held that position continuously until 1957, except for the two years he served as Commandant of the ROTC and the time he spent in service in World War II. Anderson fought in World War I and remained in the reserves where he held the rank of Colonel; he was then called back into duty during World War II.[73]

Anderson agreed to run for mayor, but he promised to only serve one term. The citizens, he contended, would not like his conservative approach to .government. It was his firm philosophy that citizens should receive little assistance from the government and that a city should not spend more than it collected. When residents inquired about his campaign slogan, Anderson replied in jest, "I promise you ham sandwich trees and lemonade springs." [74]

On April 2, 1940, Frank Anderson became College Station's second mayor. Earnest Langford and Thurmond A. Munson were elected aldermen. The election was unique in that Texas A. and M. students put up their own candidate for mayor. Although their candidate lost 460 to 12, it was the students' first venture into municipal politics. The trend would recur in later years.[75]

Anderson incorporated his philosophy in the administering of city affairs. Revenue brought in by utility sales was used in the purchasing of additional utility facilities. When the citizens wanted to change to a metered water system, the residents bought their own meters. The mayor turned down offers of federal assistance, and he was also quite proud that College Station had no bonded indebtedness while he served the city.[76]

The daily operation of city affairs had not become complex enough to warrant a full-time staff. Anderson functioned as both the mayor and city manager. He held office hours each morning. Aided by one secretary, he answered calls from citizens and tried to assist them. "If there was a polecat around, they [the citizens] would call the city office, and I would go get my gun. If there was a mad dog out, why I would go get my gun." The mayor frequently toured College Station with the city marshall to inspect city property and repair any ruptured facility.[77]

During Anderson's term in office, there was an important change in governmental procedure. After the 1941 election, the council, as authorized by general law, voted to divide the city into three wards. Two councilmen would represent each ward, and they would be elected in alternating years. The three established sections of College Station provided a convenient pattern by which the city could be divided. The area south of campus represented Ward One; Ward Two was defined by the area east of Highway 6; North Gate and any remaining part of the city made up Ward Three. Under the new system, which would take effect in the 1942 election, the council would consist of seven members rather than six. In addition to changing the election procedure, city leaders changed their title of alderman to councilman.[78]

As the 1942 election approached, Anderson, although fifty-two years old, was called to serve in World War II. Even if the colonel had decided to run for a second term as mayor, the war precluded him from doing so. Anderson recalled that during his last council meeting, he asked each councilman who they would like to have as their next mayor. Each replied that his preference was Ernest Langford.[79] Ernest Langford did indeed become mayor in 1942, and he held that prestigious title for twenty-four years. During his tenure the city grew, and its character became more fully defined. Langford and councilmen who held similar views influenced the development of College Station during a period when it evolved from a struggling town to an established city.

Chapter III

The Langford Administration, 1942 - 1966

DURING THE TWENTY-FOUR YEARS that Ernest K. Langford served as mayor of College Station, a distinct philosophy of city management emerged. Langford and the councilmen, many of whom served several terms, believed that the prime purpose of their city government was to provide basic municipal services to the academic-oriented comm-unity. City leaders were eager to utilize the knowledge and abilities of members of the learned community and to institute such progressive features of city government as a city manager system and a home-rule charter. Fiscally conservative, they expended city funds only on essential services. These officials had no desire to spend more money than was necessary, nor did they wish to increase taxes or accept assistance from other sources.

The governing philosophy, a mixture of both conservative and progressive tenets, was perhaps shaped by earlier political experiences of College Station's inhabitants and the manageable population size of the city during this period. Many city leaders and residents were employed in academic pursuits at the college, were exposed to new ideas, and were willing to experiment with innovative city management techniques. Yet, these people had also lived through the Depression, which influenced them to budget frugally.₁ Officials implemented only the necessary municipal projects, and they were able to do so because the city s population remained under 10,000 until the 1960s. As the growth rate accelerated in the later years of Langford's administration, it became apparent that the city's policies needed to be re-evaluated.

Officials Provide Progressive City Government

College Station's election of 1942 was significant for two important reasons. It marked the first time councilmen were elected by the ward system, and Ernest K. Langford began his two decade-long tenure as mayor. Langford did not set out to serve for a lengthy period. His original intent was to offer himself as a candidate for the office that became vacant when Colonel Anderson was called into military service. "Somebody had to take his [Anderson's] place," Langford explained in a 1964 interview, "and I was elected. [I] Haven't stopped since." ₂ To the office of mayor, Langford brought many talents, limitless energy, and a kind and gentle disposition. His leadership capacity profoundly influenced the development and character of College Station.

Born on May 30, 1891 in Ballinger, Ernest Langford spent his youth in two Central Texas towns of close proximity, Briggs and Bertram in Burnet County.₃ As Langford grew up, he became acutely aware of the concern of neighbor for neighbor present in the fabric of small communities and the sharing of joys and sorrows. This left an indelible impression on him.

Encouraged by his parents, he studied architecture at Texas A. and M. College. On September 19, 1909, Langford took the Houston and Texas Central to the school unaware that his lifework would be intertwined with the college and the town that college spawned. "When Langford stepped off the train at the depot ... he found cotton fields, pasture, and the site of the future city waiting."[4]

After graduating from Texas A. and M. in 1913, Langford served as apprentice under an architect in Austin for two years. In 1915 Langford was employed with the rank of instructor in the Department of Drawing at Texas A. and M. Three years later, he accepted a teaching position at the University of Illinois where he also received a master's degree in architecture. Langford returned to Texas A. and M. in 1925 as a full professor in the Architecture Department, and 1929 he became head of the department.[5]

Under Langford's twenty-seven year guidance, the Architecture Department expanded and improved. The department instituted a five-year program which received accreditation by the Association of Collegiate Schools of Architecture and the National Architectural Accrediting Board. During this period Langford also achieved professional recognition. He became a member of the American Institute of Architects (AIA), served on the board of directors of the Texas Society of Architects, and received one of the highest honors of the profession when he was elected a fellow in the AIA.[6]

For a period of fifteen years, Langford devoted his time both to the management of the Architecture Department and to his duties as mayor of College Station. While both positions required an inordinate amount of time, Langford enjoyed the work that each job entailed. Certain characteristics of the architectural profession were also present in municipal government. Langford explained in a 1961 newspaper interview that "both fields call for a love of creating something and watching it grow and develop."[7]

One of the goals of the council during Langford's administration was to provide the best possible government for the community — one that ran efficiently, was responsive to residents' needs, and encouraged citizen participation. With the demand that their full-time occupations made on them, officials did not feel they could effectively perform all necessary municipal duties. This realization perhaps crystallized when it was discovered that the city's financial records had not been properly recorded.[8]

As early as 1942, the council became interested in adopting a procedure similar to the council-manager form of government. This method of municipal organization provided for the appointment of a nonpartisan administrator who would manage city affairs and carry out policies established by the council. The mayor and councilmen would serve the city in an advisory capacity.

The city manager concept of government was introduced as part of the urban reform movement that swept the nation at the turn of the century. It was first utilized in the small city of Staunton, Virginia in 1908. Designed to answer citizen demand for efficient city management, the system appeared successful.[9] Scholars at Texas A. and M. studied municipal reforms, and beginning in the mid1920s, the Civil Engineering Department offered graduate and undergraduate courses in city management, including instruction on the city manager concept.[10] Joseph Orr, a professor of that department and a councilman from 1939 to 1966, taught municipal administration courses for many years and was a strong advocate of the city manager program for College Station. Most, if not all, of the members of the council agreed that a city manager would be desirable.

One significant factor precluded College Station from establishing a council-manager form of government. The Revised Civil Statutes of Texas made no provision for the employment of a city manager by general law cities. In order to fulfill their needs, the council created in late 1942 the full-time position of business manager to essentially function as would a city manager.[11] J. Garland Brown served as the first business manager for a month, but in November 1942 Councilman Lloyd Smith took a leave of absence from his elective post and assumed the duties.[12]

During the 1943 legislative session, the Texas Legislature authorized a bill to allow cities with a population of fewer than 5,000 to adopt, through municipal elections, the council-manager form of government. On April 4, 1944, College Station citizens gave their approval, and Lloyd Smith, who retained his former duties, became College Station's first city manager. College Station was the first general law city in Texas to employ a city manager.[13]

Along with the installation of a city manager, Langford and the council employed other measures to enhance the responsiveness of city government. Committees of citizens, such as the Advisory Committee, Sanitary Conditions Committee, and the Human Relations Council, were created to assist the public officials.[14] City leaders frequently arranged dinners with residents who represented various areas and businesses of the city. The dinners provided the council with an opportunity to allow citizens to air problems and to discuss possible solutions. [15] At least once a year the council held town meetings in the gymnasium of the high school to review major city projects and future plans.[16]

In December 1947 residents celebrated the opening of College Station's first city hall. Although the city office had moved and expanded in 1942 from one room at North Gate to two rooms in the Burgess building Southside, officials were delighted to have their own building for transacting city business. The modern one-story structure, designed by architecture students under Langford's guidance, was located in the North Gate area across Wellborn Highway adjacent to the railroad tracks. The building housed office spaces for city personnel, a warehouse, and a council chamber for monthly meetings.[17]

The new city hall proved to be a boon for College Station's community activities. Civic organizations such as the College Station Development Association and Chamber of Commerce, and the Kiwanis Club were encouraged to use the council room for their meetings.[18] In 1948 city leaders held College Station's first annual Christmas Open House in the council room.[19] The following year the Kiwanis Club sponsored the first student government day; high school students assumed the roles of city officials and participated in municipal operations.[20]

Although city leaders worked to develop College Station into a model municipality, the community displayed one significant flaw. Many citizens apparently were not concerned with the election process or were satisfied with the performance of their municipal leaders. Through the 1940s and early 50s, residents were content to retain men in office, and at election time incumbents met with little or no competition. Voter turnout for elections was consistently low.[21] Usually fewer than 100 residents in each ward voted for their choice of councilman; office seekers in the small

Ward Three easily won with only twenty votes.

Langford faced only one opponent during his entire lengthy tenure, in the 1946 election. Using the slogan, "Build College Station Now," Ralph Steen, a professor in the Department of History, ran for mayor with the desire to generate city growth. His platform included encouraging commercial development, expanding educational and recreational programs, establishing self-sufficiency while cooperating closely with Bryan, and limiting the tenure of mayor to two terms so as to keep office holders alert.[22]

Langford, perhaps because of his close ties with small communities in his past, was less concerned with stimulating commercial growth than he was with providing services to residents. Even though Langford was the incumbent, he won re-election by the slim margin of nineteen votes. Throughout the rest of Langford's political career, no other person chose to run against him.

While the mayoral position was not challenged again during the Langford period, citizens began taking an interest in the election of councilmen in the late 1950s. More people ran for office, more residents cast their votes, and the increase in competition resulted in closer races. Residents in Ward Three, however, remained relatively inactive.

The city witnessed some growth to the north, east, and south during the 1940s. College Station's status as a general law city, however, limited officials' ability to annex territory. Without its own city charter, the council could only annex property in areas where residents had petitioned for inclusion inside the city limits. This restriction frustrated officials because they could not prevent Bryan from absorbing territory in close proximity to College Station.

In April 1951 there existed, according to the *Battalion*, a "war of annexation" between College Station and Bryan. Bryan had annexed several parcels of land to the south so that the boundaries of the two cities were drawing together. Although Bryan's charter made the annexation process easier for its officials, the College Station council managed to include 150 acres in the city limits before a northern border was permanently established. The council approved the annexation petition of residents living in an area northeast of the city the night before the Bryan council was to meet to annex the same tract. College Station officials also annexed the Tauber property adjacent to North Gate.[23]

This annexation conflict encouraged city leaders to question the concept of home rule government for College Station. Through a state constitutional amendment of 1912, Texas cities with at least 5,000 inhabitants had the legal right to compose and amend their own charters. Introduced as a facet of the urban reform movement, this "home rule amendment," it was believed, would allow cities to directly govern their citizens and thus, better meet individual needs. Home rule cities could determine their own governmental organization of government and utilize options not available to general law cities.[24]

Strongly motivated by the liberal annexation powers accessible to home rule cities, city leaders were eager to adopt a charter for College Station. When the 1950 Census recorded College Station's population at 7,268, the council organized a charter commission.[25] The commission, consisting of eighteen civic leaders, met for the first time in April 1951. Under the leadership of Ernest Langford, members of the commission discussed matters to be incorporated into the charter and appointed Joseph Orr, Sol Wright, and Howard Badgett as a subcommittee to handle the finer details of drafting the document.[26]

The proposed charter created a municipal organization similar to the one that was already in operation. It retained the council-manager form of government. An elected mayor was considered the head of the government although he had no administrative duties. His vote carried the same weight as the vote of other council members, and he had no veto power. The council, the legislative body of the city, consisted of the mayor and six representatives from the community. As before, councilmen were elected by the ward system for two-year terms. The city manager, appointed by the council, was responsible for preparing an annual budget, reporting on the financial and administrative activities of the city, and proposing plans for future development. While the city manager was a full-time, salaried employee of the city, neither the mayor or the councilmen received compensation for their services.[27]

The charter would also grant officials more control over the city's annexation process. The council could extend the city limits if petitioned by a majority of qualified voters in an area, or they could annex territory by ordinance with or without the consent of inhabitants.[28] City leaders believed that this provision would allow them to develop College Station in a more orderly fashion.

Framers of the charter also incorporated new methods of direct citizen participation in their municipal government. College Station residents could utilize the initiative to propose ordinances, the referendum to approve or reject at the polls ordinances passed by council, and the recall to remove elected city officials.[29]

On November 9, 1951, the commission submitted the final draft of the charter to the council. After copies of the document were distributed to qualified voters, a special election was held on January 8, 1952. College Station residents voted 220 to 11 to adopt the charter.[30] Officials and citizens were elated that the city was operating at last under the directive of its own laws.

In June 1952 the council appointed Ran Boswell as city manager of College Station. Following Lloyd Smith, Francis Vaughn, and Raymond Rogers in the position, Boswell became the fourth administrative head of the city. He had not intended to work in municipal administration, but came into the profession by accident. After moving to Bryan in 1932, Boswell and his father operated a 7·Up Bottling Company at a time when the drink was virtually unknown. After selling the business in 1945, Boswell found temporary employment with College Station to straighten out financial records. He remained with the city, serving as assistant city secretary and tax collector.[31] Boswell then accepted the position of city manager with little inkling that he would serve in that capacity for twenty-two years. The length of his tenure as well as that of Mayor Langford 's exemplified the stability of city government during this period.

Extending City Services and Facilities

In addition to providing a responsive government, College Station officials desired to furnish residents with adequate utility systems, protective services, and other municipal amenities. They approached these responsibilities with hopes of maintaining a moderate budget and utilizing campus facilities when possible. Even so, officials realized that they would have to subject the city to bonded indebtedness. During Langford's administration the council on three occasions asked the residents for authority to issue bonds, and each time the constituents gave their support. The city's first bond election was held in 1946; voters approved $100,000 of bonded indebtedness for sewer, water, and electric extensions. A $200,000 bond proposal passed in 1950 for additional extensions and, in 1954, voters authorized $300,000 worth of bonds solely for the construction of a sewer waste disposal system.32

One important priority for the council was municipal ownership of all utility distribution systems in the city. While College Station had purchased privately owned systems and had established the policy that facilities in newly annexed areas automatically became city property, the REA lines in College Hills still belonged to Bryan. College Station officials entered negotiations in 1946 for the power lines, and the Bryan council agreed to set a valuation on the equipment.33 Four years later, however, the lines still remained in Bryan's possession. Unable to control rates in College Hills and tired of seeing residents' money going to Bryan, the council decided to erect their own lines, and contacted Brazos River Transmission Electric Cooperative about supplying service to the area.34

Stirred by these developments, Bryan offered to sell the REA lines in October 1950. The offer included two conditions: College Station would have to construct auxiliary lines around the city to serve REA patrons living outside the city limits, and College Station must buy power from Bryan, charging its residents the same rate that Bryan had set for its customers.35

The two cities did not immediately reach an agreement on the sale of the facilities. College Station officials agreed to build auxiliary lines, but they wanted to be able to determine their own electric rates. Finally, on March 12, 1951, a contract acceptable to both parties was concluded, and College Station purchased the REA lines for $38,109, using funds from the 1950 bond election. Mayor Langford proclaimed the purchase "the best money the city had spent during its ten years of existence." He speculated that an additional $1500 a month

would be added to the city's treasury in the form of electric bill payments.36

By the 1950s College Station's electric and water systerms met the needs of her residents. The sewer facilities, however, presented a problem. Bryan and College Station worked together in 1949 to lay sewer lines in the North Gate area, and effluent from that section went to Bryan's new sewer treatment plant.37

The rest of the sewage in College Station went to filter beds which were owned by F. B. Clark and had been utilized since the city's inception.38 This arrangement was inadequate and did not serve all the residents. The council, therefore, made a considerable commitment; they decided to construct their own sewerage disposal and treatment plant, the city's first major facility.

On December 1, 1954, voters overwhelmingly approved the $300,000 bond proposal necessary to finance the project. Appreciating the confidence shown by the electorate, Langford assured residents that every lot in the city would have access to a sewer line and that the system would service the city's needs for at least twenty-five years. Boswell described the facilities as "the finest system for any town this size." 39 The city contracted with the E. E. Farrow Company for construction of the plant, and by May 1956 the new facility went into operation.40

Influenced by the size and character of the city and by the availability of A. and M.'s facilities, the council turned to budgeting items for additional services. For fire protection, College Station continued to rely on the volunteer force of A. and M. employees, and for equipment, on Texas Fireman's Training School at the college. Annual fire protection expenditures included insurance fees on men and equipment, salaries, charges for use of the truck in the ever.t of a fire, and the cost of tuition to send one fireman to Fireman's Training School each summer. Since the college had all the necessary facilities, College Station enjoyed low key insurance ratings for several years.[41]

The State Fire Insurance Committee, however, recommended in 1957 and again in 1960 that College Station build its own fire station, construct a water tower, and employ full-time firemen. Although plans to implement these items were set in motion in the early 1960s, very little materialized while Langford was mayor. The council did hire Virgil B. Phipps as the city's first full-time paid fire chief in 1960.[42]

College Station's police force also remained small during the Langford era. For ten years the city marshall, later renamed chief of police, served as the main peacekeeping authority. Campus patrolmen were considered deputy city marshalls although they were rarely called upon for service. In 1949 the council authorized the purchase of a patrol car for Chief of Police Lee Norwood. A second police officer was employed to patrol the city, especially the business district, during the nighttime hours.[43] Three additional men were added to the force in 1956.[44]

As College Station matured, residents welcomed additional amenities. One of the earliest ancillary facilities to be organized, with the hearty endorsement of the community, was the city's first bank. A group of 1 05 petitioners applied for and received a charter from the State Banking Commission in November 1945.[45] College Station Bank opened its doors on May 1, 1946 in a small, two-roomed, wooden building at North Gate, and the council authorized the transfer of the city's banking business from Bryan to College Station. Residents enjoyed having the lending institution in their town not only because it served their financial needs, but also because it provided a convenient place for monetary exchange.[46]

Unfortunately, within two years the small bank encountered difficulties. The executive vice president was unable to control the bank's loans, and soon the institution was without capital. The bank briefly stopped operation in 1948, but with the support of the community, it was reorganized that same year. The institution became a national bank in the next decade, changing its title to University National Bank.[47]

In the late 1940s, College Station obtained land for a city cemetery. The only cemetery available to the community before that time was the one established on the south side of Texas A. and M. campus at the turn of the century. When the cemetery was moved west across the railroad tracks to make room for building expansion, people stopped using it. During a 1946 town meeting, residents passed a resolution urging the council to acquire property for a city cemetery. At the end of the year, the council authorized the printing of cemetery warrants in the amount of $10,000 for that purpose.[48]

College Station subsequently purchased thirty-one acres from Victor Boriski for the cemetery. The tract, two miles south of the college, included the four-acre cemetery deeded to the Methodist Church in 1870 to be used by Shiloh residents. The Methodist Conference turned the property over to College Station on the condition that it would continue to be used for burial purposes. On February 1, 1948, the picturesque acreage, which contained a small lake and would later be declared a wildflower preserve, was dedicated as the College Station City Cemetery.[49]

With the passage of a school bond election in the amount of $100,000, the school district planned to construct a new high school. Superintendent A. M. Whitis and school board member Clarence A.

Bonnen traveled throughout Texas to inspect various high schools so that they could get an idea of what facility or design could best be utilized in their structure. The new high school, located west of the existing school buildings, began operation in 1949. Lincoln School, the Negro facility located on the southern limits of the city, was also opened that year.[50] [50]

The new high school gave citizens an opportunity to organize what might be considered the city's first library. Urged by the president of the Development Association, the council and school officials discussed the possibility of making the school facility a city-school library and employing a librarian for the entire year. The council appropriated money to buy current fiction and books for young children. Councilman Howard Badgett and City Attorney Justus Wheeler Barger pledged to donate more than 100 books, and the Kiwanis Club sponsored a book drive.[51] Although the community was very optimistic about the city-school library, the program never really crystallized. Residents relied on the college or Bryan Public Library leaving the high school's library to be used mainly by students.

Other than creating a Parks Board, the council gave little attention to the development of parks or a recreational program during the first decade of the city's existence. With purchases of land from F. B. Clark and Hershel Burgess, the council established the first city park in 1947. The property, land which surrounded and included the drained College Park Lake, because known as Dexter Park and was later renamed Brison Park.[52] The residents, however, wanted more. In 1953 a large group of citizens, utilizing their newly-attained charter privileges, suggested a possible referendum which, if passed, would establish a Recreation Board. The board would operate with a budget funded by an increase in taxes.[53]

Rather than admit the proposal to a vote, Mayor Langford, with the approval of the council, appointed a five-man Recreation Board.[54] A recreation fund account was created which would receive appropriations each year. The board's duties included administering the parks and developing a recreational program with major emphasis on youth activities.[55] Within a short period of time, the board sponsored programs in swimming, tennis, golf, and little league baseball, and arranged city picnics. Most of the programs were possible, however, only because Texas A. and M. officials allowed the city to use the college's recreational facilities.

Citizens were always interested in projects which would make their community more attractive. Although the council supported proposals made by various civic groups, they could offer little financial assistance. In 1958 Councilman David A. Anderson recommended an innovative plan for the city to participate in which would cost very little. Since the sewerage plant had the right components, such as light, water and fertilizer, to serve as a nursery, Anderson suggested that tree seedlings be planted there which when grown could be placed in different sections of the community.[56]

The council wholeheartedly concurred. In March city employees tilled and bedded the soil and planted 300 seedlings which included specimens of pine, cedar, holly bay, live oak, magnolia, and pyracantha.[57] The trees were eventually planted in parks, along streets, and in individual yards. When first conceived, the plan was designated a standing operation of the city; yet, over a period of years, the practice, without explanation, was discontinued.

For the first fifteen years of Langford's tenure, College Station operated and developed with few complications. The year 1957, however, proved to be a turning point for his administration. College Station had reached a level of growth that mandated that if the city was to continue to operate productively, its development would require more planning, more governmental involvement, and an increase in municipal expenditures. College Station was at the threshold of accelerated growth, and the adjustments made in the last years of Langford's administration were important in making the transition from a quiet college town to an expanding city.

The City Faces New Challenges

During the next nine years, the tasks the council encountered presented two problems: the need for more capital outlay than the city could wisely expend, and a need to establish an organized method of municipal planning. One of the first issues that brought these problems into focus was the street improvement program of the late 1950s.

The streets of College Station had deteriorated to such a condition by 1957 that citizens were demanding a full-scale renovation program. Hired by the city to evaluate the situation, Spencer J. Buchanan reported in the November 1957 council meeting that the older streets in College Station were seriously cracked and much of the base had been washed away. He expressed his amazement that citizens traveled on those roads at all.[58]

Buchanan recommended that the city repave, curb, and gutter the roads, absorbing one-third of the cost while assessing owners on each side of the street one-third. He also explained that the project could be financed by the passage of a $500,000 bond proposal which would allow the project to be completed in its entirety, or the city could adopt a pay-as-you-go system. Ernest Brown, representative from Moroney,

Beissner and Company, the firm which financed College Station's Bonds, discouraged the use of the bond proposal. The assessed valuation of College Station, he explained, was inadequate to support $500,000 in bonds. The city would have to double its property valuations.[59]

City officials discussed the various street improvement alternatives with citizens. Mayor Langford appeared before civic organizations and listened to the residents' opinions. Joe Orr sent a letter to his Ward One constituents in which he presented several improvement options. He also stressed the seriousness of College Station's financial situation considering the other issues that required attention. Besides street repair, College Station needed such facilities as a water tower, a police and fire station, a new city hall, and an underpass at the intersection of FM 60 and the railroad tracks near North Gate.[60]

By March 1958 council had resolved that they would not hold a bond election, but rather finance a street improvement program on a pay-as-you-go basis. Officials spent the next few months trying to establish a system under which to operate. They decided that when seventy percent of the residents agreed to pay their portion of the repair of their streets, a petition with the appropriate number of signatures should be submitted to the council. Residents could also opt for curbs and gutters. The council would establish the priority of streets to be reconstructed, and the work would begin when funds became available.[61] Not all citizens were content with the city's approach to the street improvement program. Many believed that the proposed system would take too long and that the value of College Station's property would significantly decline. During the November 24, 1958, council meeting, a group led by Fred Farrar presented a petition containing 268 signatures which asked council to call a

$500,000 bond election. If passed, $350,000 could be used for street repair, and $150,000 could be spent on a water tower, fire station, and new city hall. Farrar asserted that the council might not be in touch with the residents' wishes. "We don't think," he explained, "that the council really knows what the citizens want. What we want is some good streets. The town belongs to the people and the people are ready for some new streets."[62]

Although officials were willing to hold the election, they were concerned about the financial implications. The passage of the bond election would place College Station in eighty percent of its debt limit.[63] Regardless, the council set February 17, 1959, as the date for the $350,000 street improvement bond election. Joe Orr, who made the motion for the election, explained his philosophy:

I am making this motion not because I think the election should be held or that it is desired. However, anytime a group of 265 of our citizens petition us to call an election, I think we should grant them that privilege. Frankly, I think this council is still unanimous in its previous stand to pay for our street improvements on a pay-as-you-go basis. The state, the federal government is in financial trouble, and some of our nearby towns are in financial trouble. If we can stay out of financial trouble, I believe we should government is in financial trouble.[64]

On February 17, 1959, the first bond election demanded by citizens in the history of College Station was held. In a record voter turnout, the proposal was defeated by a four to one margin. Residents cast 937 votes; the previous high had been in the 1958 regular city election where 516 votes were cast.[65] The election reinforced the council's decision to continue to spend prudently. Yet, it also emphasized the need

for long-range planning. Had officials approached the street problems sooner, citizens might not have called for the bond election.

College Station invested in her first long-range planning project in the late 1950s. The project was not exclusive to the city; it was inaugurated to coordinate the development of Texas A. and M. College, College Station, and Bryan within Brazos County. Stimulated by an increase in college enrollment, thirty-two county-wide leaders met on February 19, 1957, at the campus Memorial Student Center to discuss provisions for orderly growth. These men established the Brazos County Planning Commission, and appointed a five-man executive committee, headed by Robert B. Butler, to oversee the project.[66]

Since Bryan and College Station were growing in parallel directions to the south and east, the committee decided in October 1957 to engage the Bryan consulting firm of Caudill, Rowlett, Scott and Associates to help compile a study which would supervise the growth in the county. The plan would include guidance on future expansion of utilities, streets, business districts, highways, parks, and other facilities. The four entities agreed to share the cost of the study which was estimated at $54,000. Although a grant available from the federal government could finance one-half the cost of the project, leaders decided not to pursue that course of action. Local funding, as expressed by Langford, would insure that no strings would be attached.[67]

The following year the Planning Commission discussed the possibility of developing their organization into a non-pro fit corporation. First suggested by College Station City Attorney, Clarence E. Dillon, the proposed corporation would have more latitude to accomplish the commission's goals. It would be able to make contracts, enter into negotiations, and conduct business transactions. It was anticipated that the corporation would be able to obtain facilities for the Brazos area that the individual cities or the college alone could not.[68]

The Brazos Area Planning Corporation, considered a pioneering effort, was the first non-profit corporation of its type to be established in Texas.[69] Under its auspices the Brazos Area Plan was adopted. The plan offered profitable guidelines for the community. Interest in the corporation, however, waned by the mid-1960s. Leaders soon concentrated more heavily on the planning of their individual communities than the whole Brazos County.

During the early 1960s, College Station officials focused their attention on accommodating the growth of their own city. The Planning and Zoning Committees had been combined into one in 1958, giving it more ability to direct development.[70] The council bought six lots facing Highway 6 in the College Hills Estates subdivision as a site for a future city hall complex, and they appointed a committee to determine what facilities would be included in the complex.[71]

With the urging of Councilman D. A. Anderson, the Parks Committee was reactivated in 1963. Using the Brazos Area Plan as a point of reference, the committee was to plan for the development of parks in the city and make recommendations for improvements to the council.[72] The Recreation Council began a long-range study in July 1964 to identify the recreational needs of the community for the next twenty-five years. They proposed at that time the acquisition of twenty-five acres behind the cemetery for use as a city park.[73]

One important issue that officials analyzed was the improvement of the city's traffic network. College Station needed more east-west thoroughfares and more streets that would aid traffic flow into Byran. Officials decided in 1965 to extend

Jersey, a major east-west road, to Easterwood Airport. Suggestions were made to open up the County Road which ran by Lincoln School from Highway 6 to Wellborn Road and to connect Lincoln Street to Bryan's East 29th Street.[74] The council also agreed to contribute the city's share of the construction cost of the Highway 6 Bypasss [75]

One of the biggest transportation concerns that the council faced was the construction of an underpass at the intersection of FM 60, also known as Sulphur Springs Road and later renamed University Drive, and the Southern Pacific and Missouri Pacific railroad tracks. As early as 1957, the District Engineer of the State Highway Commission, C. B. Thames, proposed the idea to the city. If College Station would donate the right-of-way and pay the cost of utility adjustments, the state would coordinate the consolidation of the railroad tracks and build the under-pass.[76] The city tentatively agreed to financially support the plans in 1961 with the understanding that Brazos County would pay one-fourth of the condemnation fees. In 1964 Thames urged the city to begin right-of-way proceedings because the project was ready to enter the construction phase.[77]

College Station, however, encountered difficulties which threatened to prevent the fruition of the project. At first, the county was not willing to absorb twenty-five39 percent of the condemnation fees, and College Station officials were not sure they could cover the total cost. Within a short period of time, the county consented to uphold its previous agreement.[78] Secondly, Alton Boyett, a College Station councilman, and his nephew, Jack Boyett, were dissatisfied with the condemnation assessments of their property. Their decision to take their cases to court impeded the acquisition of all right-of-way properties. Unable to start construction, the Texas

Highway Department considered diverting the funds to other projects.79

Fortunately, the county was able to find satisfactory solutions to the last of the condemnation suits on March 8, 1965. The state immediately began consolidation of the railroad tracks. Construction on the underpass was slated to start in July, and it was estimated that it would be completed within fifteen months.80

Although officials and residents enjoyed their close-knit residential community, College Station had reached the stage where it had become advantageous to encourage commercial development and the establishment of light industry. Such facilities augmented tax revenues and thus provided extra funds for the financing of municipal projects. College Station had witnessed some commercial growth in various sections of the city. Shopping centers were in the process of construction at Redmond Terrace and along the north side of the campus at the intersection of Sulphur Springs Road and South College Avenue. City officials had also attended ground breaking ceremonies for the Ramada Inn in 1962.

Council members asked the Chamber of Commerce in 1965 to concentrate on attracting light industry to the city. City leaders were especially interested in securing industry that would harmonize with the research conducted at the university. An Industrial Development Committee was created that same year for the purpose of exploring the possibility of establishing an industrial area adjacent to or within city limits.81

Mayor Langford, who became seventy-six in 1966, had always wanted College Station to grow and to prosper. Yet, because of his love for the warmth inherent in a small community, he did not desire the city to develop beyond a "college town with a restful atmosphere." Since it was imperative

that College Station continue to grow, Langford believed that other civic leaders could better guide the future expansion of the town. On January 24, 1966 Langford informed the council that he would not seek re-election. He also emphasized that he was still vitally interested in the growth and development of College Station. That same night David A. Anderson and Councilman Theo R. Holleman announced their intentions to run for mayor.82

College Station officials held an appreciation dinner for the city's "greatest citizen" on June 1, 1966. Friends and fellow council members made speeches, thanking Langford for his twenty-eight years of service to the city. Fred Brison, who would serve as councilman and briefly as the mayor in the future, described the gratitude expressed at the event.

After twenty four years as mayor of College Station, 200 friends gathered to honor him [Langford] upon his retirement from that office. He was reminded at that happy time that on twelve prevwus dates, representing twenty four years, the people of College Station had, in their wisdom, gone to the ballot box to express their confuience in the leadership which he would provide. He was elected ... and re-elected without ever a platform or a pudge or a promise, but only with the unspoken assurance of the integrity and famileys and will to do good that are a part of the Langford heritage.81

The Langford era had come to an end. Much had been accomplished; yet much lay ahead for future leaders.

Chapter IV

A New Direction, 1966-1974

PRIMARILY DUE TO an expansion program initiated at Texas A. and M. College, College Station entered a dynamic period of development beginning in the late 1960s. College officials, after evaluating the school's academic program in 1961, adopted measures that stimulated the growth of both the college and the city. With hopes of attaining national recognition, officials upgraded academic and faculty standards and encouraged the enrollment of more students. In 1963 the college admitted women on a limited basis, and by 1965 students were no longer required to participate in the ROTC program. The Board of Directors implemented an S85 million building program, which included a six million dollar cyclotron complex, to complement the broadened curriculum. The institution also changed its name; Texas A. and M. College became known as Texas A&M University.[1]

Officials had not fully envisioned the rapid rate of expansion that followed. Between 1965 and 1975, student enrollment more than doubled, escalating from 9,521 to 25,247.[2] The ensuing changes were exciting for the city as well as the university. The college's new program attracted an increasing number of professionally educated people, encouraged future development of research facilities in the community, and provided jobs for citizens.

The Bryan-College Station community was recognized as the main growth center for the Brazos Valley. A significant change, however, was the movement of major business activity out of downtown Bryan toward the university.[3]
. Evidence of growth soon became visible in College Station the form of new stores, restaurants, and service centers. The number of apartments mushroomed from fewer than 100 in 1963 to more than 2,900 units ten years later.[4] City leaders and residents alike realized the need to direct this expansion. Not only was planning necessary to insure provision for adequate municipal facilities, but also to preserve the city's neighborhoods. In the early 1970s the council began to prepare College Station's first comprehensive plan for development.

During this period of the city's history, more so than previous periods, College Station reflected events that were developing on the national level. At a time when the federal government became more involved in local affairs, College Station residents elected David A. Anderson as mayor. He sought to extend the role of city government. Anderson believed that the mayor should be a strong administrator, and he took an active part in making the government an efficient operation.

College Station mirrored national issues in other ways. Reversing their previous attitude, the council applied for federal funds to finance municipal projects. The school district faced the matter of integration, and city officials, especially Mayor Anderson, took a new interest in the problems of the Negro community. College Station men also served in Viet Nam; two soldiers from the area became prisoners of war.

In the midst of the invigorating expansion, a lawsuit, brought against College Station, temporarily limited city activities. Although College Station was in the process of being transformed from a college-oriented small town to several municipal projects were seriously hampered, the city withstood the crisis and continued to develop. a major central Texas city. City leaders began charting the new course in the mid·1960s.

A New Mayor Takes Office

For the first time in twenty years, the 1966 municipal election offered voters a choice of candidates for the position of mayor. David A. Anderson, employed with the Texas Forest Service, and Theo R. "Nikkie" Holleman, a professor in the Architecture Department, ran for the office Ernest Langford vacated. The electorate was almost equally divided. In the April 5, 1966 election, which had a lower voter turnout than expected, Anderson received 437 votes to Holleman's 403.[5] Anderson accepted the honor with "deep humility" and assured the citizens that the council was ready to confront the city's many challenges.[6]

David A. Anderson, affectionately known as "Andy," was quite familiar with the procedures of governmental organizations. He had worked for federal and state agencies and had previously served on the city council. Born in Pittston, Pennsylvania, Anderson was graduated from Pennsylvania State University in 1934 with a degree in forestry. Initially employed by the United States Department of Agriculture, he joined the Texas Forest Service in May 1936 and moved to College Station in 1939. Anderson represented Ward Two on the city council for the years 1957 to 1963 and was appointed to the Planning and Zoning Committee for a two-year term in 1963. With encouragement from his former ward constituents, Anderson presented himself as a candidate for mayor in 1966. At the time of his election, Anderson was head of the Information and Education Department of the Texas Forest Service on the Texas A&M campus.[7]

Anderson immediately introduced a new philosophy of government to College Station. He assumed an active role in municipal operations, inspecting facilities, formulating new projects, and listening to citizens' concerns. Intent on establishing the individuality of College Station, he expressed his displeasure with the "Bryan-College Station community" label and suggested acquiring a separate chamber of commerce and city newspaper.[8] Anderson was most eager to stimulate growth. "We were no longer a little community," he explained. "We had to think big and grow big."[9]

The new mayor perceived the duties of his office to include administrative tasks customarily handled by a city manager. Since College Station had no written guidelines for employees, policies were inconsistent. Anderson studied the experiences of other municipalities and developed the city's first personnel manual in 1970.[10] Department files were not uniformly organized at city hall, making it difficult to find dated material. Anderson proposed an archival key based on the one utilized by the Texas Municipal League and National League of Cities to classify all municipal papers and correspondence.[11] His proposal, however, was never implemented.

Because he kept abreast of daily occurrences in the city, Anderson was able to inform the council of particular situations in a weekly memorandum. He discussed specific items, proposed plans and goals, and encouraged cooperation among the council members by reminding them that they were "working together as a team toward solving the problems of our city." [12] The mayor also corresponded with state and national leaders and members of the media on issues that affected College Station.

Anderson's approach to directing municipal growth was two-sided; he developed long-term projects, and he informed and involved College Station citizens. Anticipating as many future needs as possible, the mayor began the practice of charting long range goals. His suggestions revealed perceptive foresight, and many of his proposals were incorporated in the city's two comprehensive plans more recently. In an interview, Anderson explained his chief reason for proposing goals: "I wanted to see our city move." [13]

Anderson submitted his first five-year plan to the council in 1967. His "capital improvements" program included such amenities as a fire and police station, a new city park, expansion of the sewage disposal plant, and a cultural center. [14] The council implemented some of these suggested projects after the taxpayers approved the 1968 bond issue. In 1969 the mayor sent a list of his proposals to a cross-section of 100 citizens, asking them for comments, criticism, and additional input. Most residents responded. [15] Anderson's list of seventeen goals for 1971, his last year in office, focused on achieving municipal self-sufficiency. Establishing the city's own water source and generating its own electricity were among the items he enumerated. [16]

Beside surveying opinions, Anderson employed other measures to promote citizen interest in municipal affairs. During his administration officials composed and mailed to residents an annual report highlighting the city's yearly activities. The accounts were attractive and readable; the 1969 issue won an award as an outstanding city report at the Texas Municipal League conference. [17]

The mayor also greatly expanded the number of committees, and engaged more residents in community service. In the five years that he was in office, Anderson introduced more than twelve new committees. He hoped that such additional groups as the Health, Beautification, Safety, and Airport Zoning Committees plus the five commissions already established would strengthen community development. [18] Periodically, Anderson wrote to each committee, outlining goals and needs, and some groups submitted yearly evaluations of their progress to the council.

Anderson was most proud of the committee designated as the Mayor's Special Committee. It met only during his administration. Created to uplift the Negro neighborhoods, the committee consisted of nine black leaders representing different areas of town. At the request of the mayor, the members surveyed the Negro community. They questioned families about specific needs, quality of housing, financial situation, and occupational opportunity. [19]

Utilizing the results of the survey, the council implemented programs to improve existing conditions. Anderson met with Earl Rudder, president of Texas A&M University during this period, and worked on measures that increased salaries and benefits of the black university employees. [20] The city continued to work on extending Lincoln Street and the County Road which provided better access to black neighborhoods. The council also applied for a Housing and Urban Development (HUD) grant in order to subsidize a housing project for low-income families. Although forty units were originally planned, only five or six houses materialized. Negro families, perhaps because they did not want to leave familiar surroundings, were reluctant to move into the new housing.21

Officials also looked into the possibility of converting the partially damaged Lincoln School into a recreational center for the blacks. In January 1966 the Lincoln School, which housed educational facilities for Negro students, had burned. With 600 to 700 spectators hindering firefighting efforts, firemen and volunteers could not prevent severe damage. Ten classrooms were lost along with the library, principal's office, and all school records.22 A black citizen admitted to Anderson that the fire was intentionally set in order to force integration in College Station. Black schools in Bryan met similar fates.23

The school district agreed in 1968 to lease Lincoln School to College Station for recreational purposes. The city also obtained use of property adjacent to the school for an all-purpose sports field. The project was not immediately successful. Youngsters vandalized the facilities, and only after Anderson pleaded with the black community for support did the destruction diminish.24 By 1973, however, Lincoln Center offered a full-time recreational program for all College Station residents and offered such activities as basketball, softball, ping-pong, arts and crafts, and judo.25 In 1977 the center became city property.

A significant change in College Station's election procedure occurred near the end of Anderson's first mayoral term. Supported by many citizens, the mayor spearheaded a movement to revise the charter by replacing the ward system with election by place. The place system, in which representatives ran at large rather than for a specific area of town, seemed to offer a more equitable form of government. The then existing method gave to a councilman, elected by only a handful of people, the same authority as one who won the office with ten times as many votes.

College Station had faced this predicament for some time. While the number of active voters in Wards One and Two increased over the years, the population in Ward Three remained low. In the 1967 election, 321 residents in Ward One and 258 residents in Ward Two cast their votes; only 37 citizens in Ward Three went to the polls.26 Friction caused by the perceived inequality of the ward system intensified in the late 1960s. Alton P. Boyett, who had represented Ward Three since 1951, continually opposed programs that Anderson tried to initiate. Owner of an extensive amount of North Gate property, Boyett believed that the council accommodated the needs of the university and its faculty members while devoting little attention to business interests. He worked to defeat measures that conflicted with private development. Antone Rosprim, councilman from Ward Three first elected in 1961, generally supported Boyett's position.27

Officials held a charter revision election on January 13, 1968, and the provision to change to the place system passed along with six other charter amendments.28 College Station residents first elected their councilmen by place in the April 2, 1968 election. In that race Theo Holleman defeated Alton Boyett 1083 to 452 for Place Six.29 Shortly thereafter, Antone Rosprim resigned his position. Citizens also re-elected D. A. Anderson as mayor in the spring election. During his first term in office, Anderson and the Council had worked to make the government more responsive to the residents' needs. Now the mayor wanted to focus attention on bringing necessary municipal projects to fruition.

City Expansion Keeps Pace with Growth

The community's mushrooming growth intensified the need for implementation of projects that had long been in developmental stages. College Station's population increased from 11,396 to 17,676 during the decade of the 1960s, and the trend was expected to continue. Analysts estimated that the population would reach 23,000 in 1973, 27,000 in 1974, and exceed 30,000 by the end of the decade.[30] So Faced with these predictions, city officials reevaluated their philosophy towards seeking federal and state funds for municipal projects. They concluded that it was advantageous to apply for available grants in order to ease predictable financial problems. To aid the community in acquiring necessary government funds, College Station joined the Brazos Valley Development Council, an agency created to direct growth throughout the Brazos River Valley.[31]

College Station urgently needed to overhaul its original water system. Such facilities as a two million gallon water storage tank. One million gallon water tower, new transmission lines, and a high service pumping station were necessary, and officials calculated the total cost to be more than one million dollars. In March 1966 College Station applied for its first federal grant. Because the city could claim the Brazos Area Plan as its municipal development guide, the federal government approved a grant of $484,250 to be matched by municipal appropriations.[32] The council set September 17, 1966 as the date for a $600,000 bond election to finance the remaining portion of the project.

Concerned about existing conditions, citizens endorsed the largest bond election to date by a four to one margin.[33] Contracts for the new or improved facilities were let in the summer of 1967. By the following year, the pump station and ground storage tank neared completion, and thirteen miles of new water lines encircled the city. On September 27, 1968, the new water tower, which would serve the needs of the public for at least twenty years, began operation.[34]

The council also focused their attention on expanding sewer facilities. With the assistance of the Brazos Valley Development Council the city sought funds from the Economic Development Administration (EDA) for sewer extensions. One of the objectives of an EDA-sponsored grant was to insure that the funded project would provide job opportunities and services for people in underdeveloped areas. The EDA recognized Bryan-College Station as the growth center for the seven county area served by the Brazos Valley Development Council, and they awarded the city a $332,500 matching grant for sewer improvements in May 1970.[35] Officials, however, temporarily shelved the project when a lawsuit filed against the city that same year consumed their energies.

College Station residents finally witnessed the completion of the long-awaited city hall complex. When Mayor Anderson submitted his first five-year plan in 1967, calling for construction of new city offices and a combination police and fire station, he also suggested holding a bond election which would finance the proposals. The council at the time tabled the motion. During the July 24, 1967 council meeting, Joseph Orr, who had resigned from city government at the same time as Langford, presented a petition signed by 428 citizens that asked for a special election for many of the same capital improvements earlier endorsed by Anderson.[36]

The council agreed to the request, and in February 1968 voters approved an $840,000 bond election. The city employed Charles R. Watson as architect for the city hall complex, and city leaders held ground-breaking ceremonies for the new center on April 26, 1969.[37] The project which

Langford had dreamed of and initiated was constructed across from Texas A&M University along Highway 6. City officials held their first council meeting in the new building on March 9, 1970 and citizens celebrated the dedication of city hall and the police/fire station with an Open House on March 21, 1970. 38

Once the city acquired its own fire station, council members worked toward expanding their fire-fighting service to a full-time operation. Prior to the completion of the station, the city had installed its own fire alarm system and had purchased two 750-gallon-per-minute pumper fire trucks.39 In 1971 city and university officials met to discuss the details of gradually transferring all firefighting activities to the city. It was hoped that the transition could be completed within five years. Meanwhile, the city and the university would both contribute to the salary of Fire Chief E. F. Sevison, and College Station would continue to use the school's volunteers and equipment.40

The council also investigated ways to improve College Station's police and emergencies services. Anderson arranged to have officers from the Department of Public Safety evaluate the police department; this made College Station unique among Texas cities. The state officers inspected every aspect of the Police Department organization and suggested in a report valuable guidelines for future expansion.41 In May 1967 Melvin Luedke became chief of police, and at the same time the city added four more men to the force. Anderson was also instrumental in obtaining the national emergency phone number 911 for the community. College Station was one of the first cities in Texas and the Southwest to employ this service.42

The street repair program begun in 1957 continued to be a major municipal priority; officials earmarked $100,000 of the 1968 bond election monies expressly for the on-going project. Willing to try measures that might reduce the financial burden, the city agreed to participate in an experiment that utilized waste material in the reconstruction of streets. In late 1969 Dr. Douglas Bynum, research engineer at Texas A&M University, approached Mayor Anderson and City Engineer Lloyd James about his waste recycling project. Bynum proposed that he and his assistants apply an interface substance consisting of ground rubber tires, plastic jugs, and beer bottles on severely cracked streets and then cover it with the normal hot mixed topping. The professor theorized that the rubber interface would allow greater movement of the pavement without cracking and would act as a moisture barrier. If successful, the city could adopt the procedure and significantly reduce repair costs.43

Anderson agreed to support what was dubbed the "Rubber Streets" project. He viewed it as a possible solution to a nationwide problem, and also as an opportunity to realize the mutual benefits of joint city-university participation. Badly worn concrete streets in the Carter Grove subdivision, constructed without reinforcement by the developer, provided an excellent testing ground. Bynum applied the interface to a few streets, but the material did not settle as desired. Although not properly laid, the interface appeared to perform as predicted. Bynum and James discussed the possibility of placing the substance on an unconstructed street, but the project soon lost the attention of the city.44 James suffered a heart attack, and most of the council members became involved with an impending lawsuit.

During Anderson's administration, officials realized that as the city expanded so must the recreational facilities. The council and citizens discussed the possibility of building a large park and a swimming pool. Parks and Recreation became a city department in 1971, although the parks superintendent and his assistant were employed on a part-time basis, and the rest of the recreational staff worked without compensation. The new department also continued to rely heavily on university facilities.45 In order to insure future recreational areas, the council included parkland dedications in the Subdivision Ordinance. According to the ordinance, developers were required to donate a portion of their land, depending on the number of units they constructed, for park sites, or they could give the city the cash equivalent.46

Amid rapid municipal expansion, city leaders had to resolve problems of growth so that College Station would develop in the best possible manner. Earlier, city fathers employed zoning as a means of providing orderly growth. Citizens approved because they saw zoning solely as a way to protect their neighborhoods. One College Park resident explained to the city council in 1970, "Shortly after the City of College Station became incorporated, a Zoning Committee was established to make laws to protect the rights of people who had become permanent homeowners in each area." 47

During the early period of steady growth in College Station, city fathers could reasonably utilize zoning to safeguard residential areas. Yet, in the 1970s the city, if it was to progress, needed the commercial centers, apartments, and industries that were developing in the area. Residents had to adjust to the influx of these establishments even if it meant living in close proximity to them. College Station's planning tools, however, were inadequate; officials relied on an outdated zoning ordinance and map, and the city had no master plan to guide growth. Citizens' fears of indiscriminate zoning, piecemeal development, and eventual chaos were valid.

Groups of citizens attended council meetings through the latter half of 1969 to express their concern about the situation. They were suspicious about the council's closed sessions with the Planning and Zoning Commission, felt the recent zoning measures bred ill will toward the elected officials, and they demanded the adoption of a master plan. At the August council meeting, one resident revealed his anxiety about the zoning decisions. "We checked before we built and that property was zoned for single family dwellings. We thought we had some protection before we built." Another citizen, bluntly summing up the situation, exclaimed, "We are building a future cesspool." 48 Herman Brown, representing the Glade subdivision, presented a petition which succinctly related the feelings of the Glade residents:

We question that City Council is acting in good faith and expressing an honest and sincere concern for citizenry that it was elected to serve. Until current ordinances are changed, and a master plan for zoning has been prepared we can continue to expect piecemeal and spot zoning which will only benefit the developer and not the homeowner.49

The council agreed that it was time to update the zoning ordinance and to develop a comprehensive city plan. In October 1970 Ran Boswell applied to the Texas governor for a grant to fund the project. Before officials could really begin on the plan, College Station faced a lawsuit which seriously affected the city's governing body and temporarily halted municipal projects.

College Station Confronts a Crisis

Beginning in the summer of 1970, officers of the court examined the meaning of Sections 33 and 40 in Article 16 of the Texas State Constitution and its implications for College Station and other Texas cities. A lawsuit filed by Alton P. Boyett, a College

Station councilman for seventeen years, questioned the right of council members who were employed by Texas A&M University to receive their salaries from the state while serving in elected positions. Sections 33 and 40 prohibited payment of state warrants to employees holding another office of "honor, trust or profit." The issue which College Station city fathers had faced before they began municipal operations was once again raised, and only after a labyrinth of court activity, legislative discussion, and a state constitutional amendment election was the dispute finally resolved. The lawsuit, instigated perhaps because of personal grievances, greatly affected not only College Station but many other cities throughout the state.

After gaining twenty-four signatures for a petition which called for more business representation on the council, Alton P. Boyett initiated legal action to remove the "university interests" from city government in June 1970. Boyett believed that recent governmental decisions had benefitted the university rather than the taxpayer. "The council," he explained when he filed the suit, "has gotten to the point where it is dominated so thoroughly by the university that the local resident and local businessman now feels he has only one representative on the council." [50] In a 1983 interview, D. A. Anderson speculated that Boyett 's actual motive behind the lawsuit was his dismay at losing his council seat in the first place system election in 1968 and being prohibited by the council from using city streets as parking areas for his proposed apartment complex at North Gate.[51]

If successful, the results of such legal action threatened the livelihood of six of the seven council members. Mayor D. A. Anderson and Councilmen Dan Davis, James Dozier, Joseph McGraw, Clifford Ransdell, and Cecil Ryan were employed by Texas A&M University; only Councilman Bill Cooley remained unaffected. Since the outcome could have serious repercussions in the city, College Station filed a class action suit in the Bryan 85th District Court on August 1, 1970 before Boyett's suit came to trial in Austin. The city asked Judge William C. Davis to decide whether the councilmen were holding more than one "civil office of emolument" as forbidden by the Texas Constitution. If they were, the city further asked the judge to declare Sections 33 and 40 unconstitutional under the United States Constitution. College Station officials wanted the court to definitely determine whether university employees could receive payment from the state while on the city council.[52]

College Station hired the Houston law firm of Baker, Botts, Shepherd and Coates, and Boyett retained Elmer Patman of Austin. The trial began on September 11, 1970. During the proceedings Patman tried to establish that the college had received special treatment from the city, such as street lighting around the perimeter of the campus, the underpass at FM 60, and the overhead walkway across Wellborn Road. He also questioned the professors as to whether they ever used their state-supplied campus offices for city business, or if their civic duties ever conflicted with their professional obligations.[53]

Frank Harmon, the lawyer handling the city's case, stressed the advantages that College Station won by having professors on its council. Ernest Brown, the city's financial advisor, confirmed that College Station received better bond ratings because of its highly qualified municipal leaders. He also emphasized that the case was detrimental to the city's ability to obtain funds for various projects. James Dozier testified that he had tried to get businessmen to run for the council but many declined because they did not want to jeopardize any business they had with the city.[54]

Davis ruled on September 23, 1970, that Texas A&:M University employees were not "officers, agents, or appointees" of the state within the meaning of Article 16 in the Texas Constitution. He emphasized that university faculty members could not formulate state law nor could they collect revenue or acquire property for the state. If determined in another court that the terms in the constitution did apply to the professors, then Davis believed Sections 33 and 40 were unconstitutional. The state constitution violated the First and Fourteenth Amendments by discriminating against a person's ability to seek a nonpaying municipal office. Davis stated, however, that his decision did not necessarily resolve the Boyett suit in the Travis court because that case sought no declaratory judgment against other university employees who might hold municipal office in the future. Boyett immediately appealed Davis' ruling to the First Court of Civil Appeals in Houston.55

Judge Herman Jones of the 53rd District Court in Travis County considered postponing Boyett's original suit until after the appellate court had reviewed the decision handed down in Bryan. He decided to go ahead with the trial, and scheduled the court date for November 10, 1970. In the meantime, several signers of Boyett's petition, who were also named co-plaintiffs in the case, reconsidered their decision. Many had not understood the actual purpose of the petition. Believing he had signed a document asking the council to re-evaluate municipal spending, Pat Callahan, manager of the Western Motel, explained that the intent of the petition was misrepresented. He expressed his apologies to city leaders in a newspaper article:

I did sign along with my neighbors a protest against government paid low {housing/ rents, high costs of this and that including the center highway stripe in front {of the
motel]. My advice to anyone in buying an insurance policy or signing a petition is don't depend on what the man says. 'Read the fine print.' With regrets to the mayor and city officials over this unfortunate delay in our city's 'forward progress'. 56

By the time the case came to trial, ten of the twenty-four petitioners had withdrawn from the suit. Proceedings in the Boyett lawsuit lasted three days with lawyers covering issues similar to those used in the class action suit heard in Bryan. On November 13, 1970, Jones stated his decision which countered the previous ruling. Jones contended that the five councilmen were violating the Texas Constitution, and thus their salaries could not be paid with state warrants. He stipulated, however, that since Anderson worked for the federally funded Texas Forest Service, he could continue to receive his salary. The university could also use local funds such as tuition fees to pay the other professors. Although it was not certain that the councilmen had to either forego their salaries or resign their posts, Dozier, who had a law degree, filed an appeal for the individual defendants with the 3rd Court of Civil Appeals in Austin. 57

Judge Jones' ruling had a widespread impact throughout Texas, affecting as many as fifty cities and towns. It not only applied to municipal officers, but also to state employees who worked with soil conservation districts, water districts, and school boards. Officials in Austin, Denton, Canyon, Waco, Commerce, Greenville, and Del Rio grappled with the problem.58

Since the professors would lose their right to appeal if they resigned from public office, Jack K. Williams, president of Texas A&M University, agreed to use local funds to pay the men's salaries. The university offered to support the city officials in this manner only until their present term expired and refused to extend the arrangement to any other employee who decided to run for a council position.59

The courts soon prohibited this temporary solution and further reduced College Station councilmen's ability to remain in office. The Houston court of appeals threw out the Bryan class action suit because it involved the same issues as the earlier Boyett case.60 On April 28, 1971, the Austin appellate court ruled that the professors could not be paid with any state funds including local monies or appropriations generated from the federal government.61

At the time of the Austin appellate court decision, only four of the original six councilmen named in Boyett's suit remained in office. Dan Davis opted not to run again when his term ended, and Joseph McGraw lost his council seat by a slim margin in the April 1971 election. Faced with their losing their means of financial support, the men considered the impact of their next course of action on their families as well the community. Four university employees had already resigned from the school board. By May 5, 1971 the council members reached their decision; Anderson and Dozier decided to remain in office while Ryan and Ransdell submitted their resignations.62

In the following emotion-filled days, the council members discussed their decisions. Dozier vowed to continue to appeal the case even to the Texas or United States Supreme Court. Anderson said that it was essential that he make sure that the city was not "torn asunder" by any premature action on his part. With sorrow, Ransdell publicly expressed his regrets. "I felt the outcome of [the suit]," he stressed, "was to disenfranchise all the people in College Station who depend on the university for their livelihood . . . I feel my resignation is,

in a way, letting them [the citizens] down." Ransdell encouraged the citizenry to stop the "bickering" because College Station was rapidly maturing and had may municipal matters to handle.63

The city utilized another avenue of approach in solving its dilemma. Urged by Anderson, Representative Bill Presnal of Bryan introduced a resolution in the Texas House that called for a constitutional amendment committee meeting to consider changing the two controversial sections in Article 16. On May 4, 1971, mayors from the cities of Denton, Canyon, Greenville and Schulenberg, as well as Mayor Anderson, testified to the hardships created by the court's recent interpretation of the constitution. Organizations such as the Texas State Teachers Association, Texas Municipal League, Texas School Board Association, and Texas Association of College Teachers also lent their support.64 The legislators eventually agreed to submit a constitutional amendment proposal to voters in the November 1972 state election.

Although encouraged by the possibility of a favorable constitutional amendment, Anderson and Dozier could not forego their salaries for an extended period of time. By the end of June, Anderson concluded that he must relinquish his office. He submitted a letter of resignation to the council on June 28, 1971, apologizing for not being able to serve his full term and expressing the distress he suffered through the proceedings. "The suit," he wrote," has been a most trying period to me and my family ... it is difficult to relate how it has affected one's peace of mind." 65 Mayor Pro-Tempore Fred Brison acted as head of College Station's government until a special mayoral election was conducted in August 1971.

James Dozier continued to battle the issue alone, exhausting all legal measures available to him. After the Texas Supreme Court upheld the lower court's ruling in the

Boyett case, Dozier decided he could no longer remain in office and on October 31, 1971, he resigned his position.[66] Anderson and his wife sent letters to Texas residents and officials urging them to vote for the amendment proposal. The proposal was approved the following November, and by the April 1973 municipal elections, professors could once again run for office.[67] The issue which caused great turmoil for College Station had been permanently resolved.

The Hervey Administration

During 1971, College Station had held four municipal elections, the regular spring election and three special elections. Encouraged by Anderson, retired Texas A&M professors James D. Lindsay and C. A. Bonnen ran for and won the places vacated by Ransdell and Ryan. Homer Adams captured Dozier's seat in December. When D. A. Anderson submitted his resignation as mayor, only James B. "Dick" Hervey announced his candidacy for the office. On August 17, 197 l, Hervey became the fifth elected head of College Station's government.

A native of Greenville, Texas, Hervey was the first College Station mayor to have business affiliations. He was graduated from Texas A. and M. College in 1942 and served as executive director for the university's Former Students Association for seventeen years. Shortly thereafter, he became a vice president of University National Bank. Utilizing his banking skills, Hervey helped organize the Community Savings and Loan and was appointed its president in 1966. Hervey also served four years on the Bryan-College Station Chamber of Commerce. At the time of his election, he was a member of the A&M Consolidated School Board. While publicly expressing his regrets that professors were prevented from serving on the city council, Hervey hoped he could fairly represent both university and business constituents. He outlined his main goals as furthering orderly municipal growth and attracting more businesses and light industry to the city.[68]

Soon after Hervey took office, another lawsuit was filed against College Station. Bruce Clay, a student at Texas A&M, wanted to compete for Dozier's vacated council position. He found, however, that College Station's charter required that candidates own real property in the city.[69] Hervey quickly resolved the conflict by allowing Clay's name to be placed on the ballot and by appointing a charter revision committee to make recommendations that remedied the unconstitutional clause.[70]

Although Clay did not win in the special election, he continued to strengthen the students' voice in city government. He presented a resolution, which was approved by the council that called for a conference between council members and the executive committee of the student senate in order to increase communications between the two bodies. Clay also made a significant showing in the 1972 election, losing to C.A. Bonnen by a vote of 516 to 465.[71] It was through Clay's efforts that the council established the first student polling place on campus in July 1972. [72]

Under Hervey's guidance, the council worked to extend facilities, using government grants when available and to develop a comprehensive municipal plan. The 1970 Census recorded the combined population of the Bryan, College Station area at 51,395, and thus in February 1971 the adjacent municipalities received the Standard Metropolitan Statistical Area (SMSA) designation. The SMSA certificate prompted the listing of the communities in research-oriented magazines and made them eligible for more federal funds.[73] College Station used the majority of its appropriated 1972 and 1973 revenue sharing funds to finance the earlier scheduled sewer extensions. Federal monies designated for the project in 1970 were impounded before the city could utilize them.74 By the end of Hervey's term, College Station had completed a new two million gallon waste disposal plant.

The council made substantial progress in establishing the long-awaited municipal park with swimming facilities during the early 1970s. College Station learned that beginning in the summer of 1973 its residents could not use the Texas A&M pool, and it became imperative that the city develop the proposed park. In 1973 William Fitch donated sixteen additional acres adjacent to the selected park site, and the federal Bureau of Outdoor Recreation approved a matching grant of $132,000 for the development of a pool. The city hired J.W. Wood as architect-engineer for the project, and although the budget would not allow all requested amenities to be constructed, residents soon enjoyed the availability of an Olympic-size swimming pool in their community.75 College Station's first aquatic facility, later named Adamson Municipal Pool, opened in Bee Creek Park on October 5, 1974.76

In September 1973 College Station followed the actions of forty-five other Texas cities and adopted a hotel/ motel tax. Officials planned to use the three percent tax to increase tourism.77 Early on, council members discussed donating the proceeds to the Chamber of Commerce and Texas A&M's convention fund, or to establishing the city's own tourist-convention center. Although city leaders were undecided on how to utilize the funds effectively, they believed the tax would greatly benefit the community in the future. Officials now had the financial means to sponsor creative projects which would enhance the environment of the city.

Perhaps the most important project initiated during Hervey's short tenure was the city's first comprehensive plan. In June 1972 the city accepted a 701 Planning Grant from the Texas Department of Community Affairs that financed seventy-five percent of the development of a city plan. The Bryan-based planning firm of Charles Pinnell and Associates was hired to direct the progression of the plan through three stages: preliminary objectives, recommendations for directing growth, and plan proposals and implementation.78 To help facilitate the planning process, the council organized ten citizen advisory committees, each consisting of six members and representing different geographical districts of the city.79

During the first phase, the committees surveyed the goals that residents in each section wanted to see adopted by the city. Citizens reported that while they would like an increase in shopping and entertainment facilities and light industry, they hoped College Station would remain a quiet town. They were not in favor of bringing heavy industry into the area and discouraged promoting the city's population beyond 40,000. Residents also listed their major municipal concerns as street repair, fire service, and spot zoning.80

Also in this phase, Pinnell and city leaders identified future municipal services needs. They discussed the possibility of the city drilling its own water well, negotiating a long-term electrical contract, providing low-cost housing, and establishing a network of sidewalks and bicycle paths. College Station had only made a small dent in securing adequate parkland; the city had set aside forty-five acres, but its population required at least 200 acres. Pinnell also suggested that the city separate its fire and police departments and expand the number of city employees threefold.81

Phase Two, the stage in which Pinnell and Associates made recommendations for directing growth, began in October 1973. The planners worked on a management study, a transportation analysis, and land use plans.[82] Citizens were most concerned about future land use proposals; this was the main reason they wanted a master plan. In October 1972 council members completely revised the city's original zoning ordinance, although many residents requested that the council wait and work on zoning in conjunction with the 701 Plan. Believing they could not afford to delay, the council mapped out the different zoning areas in the city and increased the types of zoning districts from five to fifteen.[83] Citizens now hoped that Ordinance 850, the city's zoning program, could be successfully integrated into the comprehensive plan.

Pinnell introduced the last phase in April 1974. At this point, specific plans focusing on city administration and organization, parks and recreation, and capital improvements were delineated. Planners also drew up a method of implementing the proposed projects.[84] The final part of the project was completed within a year, but the council did not immediately adopt the finished guide. City leaders discussed its strengths and weaknesses for the next eighteen months. The council finally accepted the Pinnell Plan in September 1976.[85] Unfortunately, by that time many of the suggestions were inapplicable or outdated, and city officials soon looked into the possibility of developing another comprehensive plan.

Ran Boswell, College Station's city manager for twenty-two years, submitted his resignation in December 1973. Six months earlier, Boswell revealed his intention to retire, and the city carefully planned for a transition. In September Boswell hired North Bardell as assistant city manager with the intention of preparing him for the city manager's position. Bardell was a graduate of Texas A&M University, receiving both Bachelor and Master of Science degrees in Civil Engineering. An associate professor of Engineering Design Graphics at Texas A&M and a member of that department for twenty years, he had also served as College Station's assistant city engineer for the previous eleven years.[86] The city council named Boswell "City Manager Emeritus" on December 15, 1973 and scheduled a retirement celebration in his honor.[87] After Bardell assumed the duties of city manager in January 1974, Boswell, whom the Eagle claimed "possibly served as the same city's manager longer than any other person in Texas," continued to be a consultant to the city.

After serving as mayor for three years, Hervey announced in February 1974 that he would not seek reelection. In a brief written report, Hervey explained his reason for relinquishing the office. "I stated I would not be a long term mayor or office seeker but would do my best while serving. That commitment has been met."[88] During Hervey's administration, the city completed a new waste disposal plant, obtained a large city park with a swimming pool, and initiated the long range 701 Plan. Most importantly, Hervey provided leadership at a crucial period in College Station's history and helped return stability to city government. Officials had shown that College Station was capable of adjusting to rapid growth and able to withstand a crisis. With these signs of strength, future leaders aimed their goal toward municipal self-sufficiency.

Chapter V

Modern City, 1974-1988

BEGINNING IN THE MIDDLE 1970s, College Station entered a fourth stage of development. As in the previous period, the city continued to expand rapidly, and policies earlier outlined aided in directing growth. Yet, during this period, College Station revealed a new dimension; the relatively young municipality made significant strides toward its goal of self.sufficiency. Leaders loosened ties with both Texas A&M University and the City of Bryan and initiated key municipal projects. The council gave financial support to a variety of community programs, but also met with more citizen confrontations. The excitement in this period is keenly evident; officials and residents alike worked to make their city a prosperous community.

Officials Strive for Self-Sufficiency

During the last half of the 1970s, the maturation of College Station became apparent in many areas of growth. A Capital Improvements Committee, first appointed in 1975, began to guide the implementation of major municipal projects. Utilizing many of the proposals suggested in the comprehensive plan, the committee established priorities and set project starting dates. To finance the expansive programs, the council presented bond elections for substantial amounts of money, and residents usually gave their approval. New

commercial establishments developed in the community as well as the city's first industries. Municipal elections also became competitive, and the new leaders were men and women eager to take action.

The first election after Mayor Hervey announced his decision not to run again for office reflected this competitiveness. In the closest mayoral election in College Station 's history, Oris M. Holt, a retired Texas A&M professor of Agriculture Education, narrowly defeated Bob Bell by a vote of 857 to 842.[1] The young Bell, manager of the KTAM-KORA radio station, received support from the business community and also captured a majority of the surprisingly large student vote in the 1974 election.[2] Throughout the remainder of the 1970s Texas A&M students continued to vote in larger numbers, offer more candidates for office, and voice their opinions in municipal government.

College Station's progression toward self-sufficiency escalated when the city began to phase out its strong reliance on Bryan's utility services. Although the city had earlier purchased water and electricity from Texas A&M, College Station now almost exclusively depended on Bryan for utilities. By 1975, however, city officials had grown dissatisfied with rates charged by Bryan. The council sent a letter of protest concerning utility increases in May 1975, but agreed to accept the assessments until Bryan submitted a new rate proposal at the first of the year.3 Meanwhile, they discussed the possibility of contracting with other distributors or constructing their own facilities to supply residents' needs. Leaders took the first initial step in that direction when they negotiated with the Whalen Corporation of Dallas to dig the city's first water well.

In order to determine whether College Station's water was potable, city officials authorized a water contract with Whalen in June 1975 to drill a well near the ground water storage site. If the project proved unsuccessful, College Station agreed to share half of the expense already incurred. If, on the other hand, the water could be used, Whalen contracted to pay all construction costs and sell the city 400,000 gallons of water a day for ten years at a cheaper rate than that being charged by Bryan.4 At the end of that time period, the equipment would become city property. To the delight of city officials, potable water was discovered, and College Station's first well began pumping water on April 12, 1976. Since the facility supplied only approximately one·third of the city's demands, officials continued to buy water from Bryan, but also initiated plans to drill two additional wells.5

The new utility rates proposed by Bryan in January 1976 greatly disturbed College Station council members. Not only were the electricity rates forty percent higher than those of a leading competitor, but the agreement also included conditions that would adversely affect College Station's ability to purchase utilities from other sources. In the current contract between the two cities which expired in January 1979, College Station had the option to buy utilities from other companies. The council, therefore, rejected the offer and asked for a new proposal with competitive electrical rates, or the city would negotiate a contract with a different distributor.6

Although Bryan wanted to continue supplying utilities to College Station, its officials believed the rate proposal represented a fair compensation for the services they provided. They explained that their city needed to increase its overall supply of revenue in order to keep a satisfactory rating with bonding companies. They further agreed to return a portion of the savings to College Station if utility expenditures were less than predicted.7 Bryan Mayor Lloyd Joyce, however, stipulated in a letter to College Station council members that if the two cities did not reach an agreement and College Station purchased power from another utility company, then Bryan would terminate all utility services, including water and sewer, when their contract expired in 1979. 8

College Station municipal leaders were uncertain that the city could provide all the necessary utility facilities and services if the contract with Bryan was indeed abrogated. They decided to present a large bond proposal to the public in the summer of 1976 which would provide the financial means for the necessary capital improvements. Mayor Lorence Bravenec, an accounting professor at Texas A&M who ran unopposed for the office in the 1976 elections, concluded that if voters approved the funds for utility expansions, then the city would view that as a mandate for change.

The $12.8 million bond election included other propositions besides the ones for utility improvements. City officials asked voters to endorse funds for street improvements, parkland acquisition, and construction of a new police station, fire substation, city warehouse, and maintenance building. They also added a proposal meant to canvass the residents' interest in a civic center. On June 29, 1976, voters affirmed each proposition and overwhelmingly supported the utility system improvements.9

Encouraged by the election results, council members immediately secured a new contract for electricity. The following day they signed an agreement with Gulf States Utilities Company which afforded partial sevice until 1979. At that time the company would then supply all power to the city. After concluding the pact, Bravenec expressed his concern about the impending break with the neighboring city. "It's with a certain amount of sadness," he remarked, "that we say farewell to Bryan."10 The complete changeover in utility services, however, was not immediate or without complications, and in some instances, Bryan impeded the progress.

Two weeks after the June bond election, city officials applied for a one million dollar matching EDA grant through the Brazos Valley Development Council to aid in the implementation of a new water system. The city planned to utilize the funds for the construction of two new wells and additional water lines. Mayor Joyce of Bryan protested to the Development Council about College Station's petition because he believed the money would be used to repeat facilities already in the area or in the planning process. Bryan had recently submitted a request for a one million dollar grant to construct an elevated storage tank which would meet local needs for ten years.11

The Development Council deferred action on College Station's application for some time. Finally the group concluded that since Bryan would not sell water separately from electricity to the city, College Station's project was not a duplication in facilities. The council agreed to send the request to the federal government with its approval, but they also decided to include Joyce's written protest.12 College Station unfortunately never received federal funds with which to develop their water program.

During the following year Bryan continued to create difficulties. In May 1977 Bryan officials filed a suit with the Public Utilities Commission for the purpose of preventing Gulf States from serving College Station. The Commission, however, denied their request.13 That September Bryan municipal leaders abrogated the joint ownership of the North Gate sewer line with College Station and announced the construction of their own complete system. City Manager Bardell determined that College Station could install a new transmission line for North Gate by 1979, but estimated that additional bond money might be required since a lift station would be essential to the project. As a possible solution to the problem, Bardell asked Bryan officials to consider creating a regional sewer authority consisting of the two cities, the county, and the university. Bryan, which had earlier suggested that College Station de-annex the North Gate area, rejected the proposal.14

Ironically, within a week after severing the partnership in the joint North Gate sewer line, Bryan councilmen seriously proposed merging the two cities into one. They emphasized that this action would avoid duplication of services and provide a united front for federal grant applications. Councilman Wayne Gibson believed it would serve the best interests of citizens in both communities, and Councilman Travis Bryan III felt Bryan residents favored the idea. "I think," he explained, "the people of Bryan would welcome a chance to unify with College Station. We could be one big happy family and solve this whole deal [with the utility systems] ... no more piecemeal remedies." 15

College Station council members, however, did not express much support for a merger. Mayor Bravenec indicated that the two cities' divergent philosophy on zoning would preclude a harmonious union, and he also stated his concern that Bryan might dominate all activities. Other College Station councilmen did not consider the proposal practical and viewed cooperation as the best way to achieve solutions to problems between the two cities.[16]

At the end of 1978, many capital improvement projects implemented to handle the change in utility service and to facilitate municipal expansion approached completion. A new waste disposal plant and the sewer line for North Gate were scheduled to begin operation in the near future. Expanded electrical amenities included an additional substation, switching station, and more feeder lines. Law enforcement personnel moved into the Police and Municipal Courts Building, and maintenance and warehouse facilities were already in use. City employees and residents enjoyed the finished addition to city hall and its spacious council chambers. Bonds approved in 1976 combined with funds from the 1978 $9.2 million bond election financed these projects.[17]

In early 1979, College Station's proposed water system was still in the construction stage. After the utility contract with Bryan expired, city leaders concluded an arrangement with Texas A&M University. Until the city completed its system, the university agreed to provide College Station with water at a reduced rate in exchange for ownership of a well expressly drilled for the school at city expense.[18] By November 1979 College Station's two new wells, located north of Bryan, were successfully completed, but it took two additional years to finish the nine million dollar water system. Officials dedicated the new facilities, which included two pump stations, a cooling tower, a three million gallon ground storage tank, and fourteen miles of transmission lines, in December 1981. Since the new system could pump 27 million gallons of water a day,

College Station had for the first time its own independent water supply.[19]

Announcements of the location of a prominent industry and the construction of a regional mall in College Station were made within a month of each other during the summer of 1979. Texas Instruments hoped to open a manufacturing facility on a 250-acre tract east of the city in early 1980.[20] Developers of the mall proposed to build a center near the East Bypass and Highway 30 which would house four major stores and more than 100 smaller shops. They expected the commercial facilities to provide 2500 new jobs for residents and to attract shoppers from all around the adjoining counties.[21] Citizens celebrated the opening of Post Oak Mall in February 1982.

These recent industrial and commercial establishments reflected a new direction in the maturation of College Station. Whereas earlier development had focused mainly around the university, officials now made a concerted effort to diversify interests in the community. Effective future expansion required that the city obtain a broader, more balanced tax base. In order to achieve that goal, the council adopted a policy of attracting industry to the city. Using funds from the hotel/motel tax, the council agreed in October 1980 to help finance the newly-formed College Station Industrial Development Foundation. Dennis H. Goehring, previously the chief executive officer at the Bank of A&M, headed the organization and many city bankers and businessmen were members. The major thrust of the foundation was to bring high-technology, electronic, and research-oriented firms into the community.[22]

College Station's desire to invite specialized industries to the area complemented its goal of attaining self sufficiency. In the early 1980s the community displayed signs of drawing closer to that objective. The city had constructed new municipal facilities, experienced increasing commercial and industrial growth, and provided its own sewer and water utility systems for its residents. Officials continued to discuss and plan for additional far-reaching projects.

Council-Community Relations

Although city leaders concentrated heavily on establishing facilities for municipal operation, they also realized the importance of an emotionally enriched community. Council members believed that the city's recreational, cultural, and social facilities needed to keep pace with the rapid growth, and during this period they initiated or provided funds for a myriad of programs. Even with the increased support for civic activities, officials encountered conflicts with various citizen groups. While the difficulties were not always easy to resolve, the experiences contained positive aspects. Citizens exercised their right to express concern about their government, and officials worked toward solutions that benefitted the community as a whole.

Since the early 1950s, residents expressed interest in a city-wide recreational program and in acquiring municipal park sites. City leaders, especially in recent years, had made significant progress toward that goal. The expansion in city parks and recreational facilities during this period, however, was phenomenal. Not only did the amount of park acreage double, but officials also sought to accommodate a variety of activities. The development of the Parks and Recreation Department reflected the growth. The parks director and department employees worked full time and worked meticulously to implement the projects. With additional funds allocated from the Bureau of Outdoor Recreation in 1974, the city added tennis courts, ball fields, and playgrounds at Bee Creek Park.[23] In September 1975 the Brazos County

Bicentennial Committee inquired about the possibility of establishing an official county arboretum at Bee Creek in conjunction with the national celebration. The council enthusiastically supported the idea and donated seventeen undeveloped acres. Citizens from both the city and county planted and labeled various species of trees and mapped out a nature trail.[24] The arboretum was ready in time for the 1976 Fourth of July festivities.

Through the late 1970s, the council continuously added land and facilities to the parks system. They changed the parkland dedication ordinance in 1975 so that developers were required to donate additional acres for neighborhood recreational areas as their total number of housing units increased.[25] The following year the city established the College Station Parks and Recreation Foundation, a trust fund created expressly for the purpose of purchasing Lincoln Center from the school district.[26] Using federal money received in December 1977, the Parks Department developed facilities at the Thomas and Oaks Parks on the east side of the city. A second municipal pool opened in Thomas Park on June 21, 1980. Its accessories included a plastic bubble dome which allowed indoor swimming during the winter months.[27]

Perhaps the Parks and Recreation Department's greatest achievement was the development of College Station Central Park. Originally, council members purchased forty-seven acres in June 1 978 near the East Bypass and Krenek Tap Road in order to provide athletic fields for the community's organized softball and soccer teams. The site also contained a large wooded expanse and a pond. The natural setting convinced parks officials to expand the facility to a multi-purpose recreational area. Tennis courts, picnic areas, playground facilities, nature trails, and a group pavilion to accommodate 300 people were included in the plans. College Station residents celebrated the completion of their largest municipal park in August 1982. The Parks Department not only decided to use Central Park as a model for future developments, but also chose to establish their office building and maintenance warehouse amid its scenic setting.28

Besides planning for recreational facilities, the council participated in various projects which they hoped would benefit the community. In 1976, they considered the feasibility of establishing bicycle lanes in several residential areas, primarily for use by college students. The Brazos Valley League of Women Voters, after conducting an eight-month study, recommended to the city that paths be striped and signs posted in subdivisions east and south of the campus. By August 1976 the proposed paths had been marked, and the city applied for federal funds to construct a more elaborate system.29 The funds, however, never materialized, and the council revised their policy in 1980. Since residents complained about the twenty-four-hour parking restriction along the paths, officials only striped such busy streets as Jersey and Southwest Parkway; all other roads were now designated with bicycle route signs which did not prohibit on -street parking.30

The council agreed in 1978 to use hotel/motel tax funds to subsidize a municipal art collection program. Organized by the Arts Council of Brazos Valley, the program, described as a "first in Texas," consisted of a statewide competition for paintings depicting College Station as it appeared in 1978.31 The Arts Council scheduled a show in March 1979; paintings were judged and prizes totaling over $13,000 were awarded. The prize-winning entries became city property and were publicly displayed.32

A county-sponsored Tourist Information Center also received financial support from the College Station City Council in January 1978 when the council appropriated $50,000 for its share of operating expenses and donated a city-owned house across from the cemetery for temporary quarters. The Information and Hospitality Center of Brazos County, the group that operated the facility, hoped to promote area tourist attractions and increase convention activity in the community.33

Although citizens had approved funds for a civic center in the 1976 bond election, city officials did not concentrate on acquiring the facility until 1979. At that time council members discussed the possibility of purchasing the old A&M Consolidated High School built in 1949 and renovating it as a community center. Representatives from various organizations, especially the senior citizens, urged the council to take action; the center would provide space for club meetings.34 In a trade with the school district, College Station received the brick structure in exchange for city-owned property near the new high school. The council spent one million dollars in renovations and additions, and the civic center, featuring six meeting rooms, a kitchen, two patios, and a large multi-purpose room, opened in June 1982.35

The first complication with citizen groups during this period occurred in 1976 and resulted in a complete revision in the city's voting procedure. Texas A&M students wanted to return to the election of officials by the ward system, and they submitted a student senate bill requesting such a measure to the council during the September 24, 1973 city meeting.36 They believed that election by wards would provide more representation for the student body in municipal affairs.

Previous charter amendments prevented the proposal from appearing on the ballot until the 1976 spring election. At that time the Charter Revision Commission offered the public an amendment with three options: retain the at-large system, establish six wards, or combine the ward/at-large programs. Ironically, permanent College Station residents who supported a change to the ward system did so because they wanted to prevent special interest groups, such as students, from gaining a majority of council positions.37

The votes tallied in the April 3, 1976, election revealed that 1,190 citizens voted for the institution of wards while 1,161 residents elected to keep the at-large system. City officials were surprised at the outcome and suggested that the complexity of the proposition caused accidental passage. At the next council meeting, council members discussed this quandary. They were confronted with the task of identifying six precincts with equal population although they had no viable population data to guide them. Since the wards would not align with county voting districts, the city would have to maintain its own voter registration lists. Councilmen estimated that the extra expense would be between $5,000 and $10,000 per year.38

Many citizens were also dismayed with the prospect of reverting back to the ward system. Former Mayor D. A. Anderson presented a petition with over 700 signatures to the council on April 27, 1976 which asked officials to contest the election. Anderson explained that the wording of the proposed charter amendment was ambiguous. He also pointed out that minority groups would not benefit from a six ward system since College Station had no area of high minority concentration.39

Concerned with the citizens' petition and their own misgivings about the election outcome, the council decided to include a straw vote on voting procedure with the June 1976 bond election. They simply asked residents to indicate whether they wanted the ward system or at-large method of election. The straw vote revealed that sixty-eight percent of the voters favored the at-large system.40 Since the city could not formally protest, Mayor Bravenec helped citizens file a suit contesting the election, and College Station City Attorney Neeley Lewis agreed to present the case. The court date was scheduled for September 9, 1976 in the 85th District Court.41

Many Texas A&M students, who earlier were pleased with the results of the charter amendment election, did not want to see the vote for the wards annulled. Three members of Texas A&M student government, Jerri Ward, Mary Ellen Martin, and Robert Harvey, conferred with Attorney Kent Caperton about a possible avenue of defense. Under Caperton's counsel, the students submitted a letter to the county courthouse, asking Judge W. C. Davis to uphold the charter revision election. Caperton also entered a plea of intervention which allowed him to present support for the ward system vote during the September 9th hearing.42

In the decision announced on October 22, 1976, Judge Davis upheld the validity of the election. Davis explained that the contestants failed to prove that irregularities affected or changed the result of the election. He believed the confusion that occurred at the polls did not stem from the wording of the amendment but from failure on the part of the voter to take sufficient time to read the entire proposal.43 City officials had no other choice but to delineate six ward boundaries, equally dividing the population, and submit themto the United States Justice Department for approval.

College Station's new ward system, which required great effort to accurately outline, did not remain in effect for long. In the April 2, 1978, municipal election, voters chose by a three to one margin to re-instate the at-large system.44 Although the Justice Department had a right to reverse the decision, College Station's homogeneous demographic makeup precluded the need for ward representation. By the next spring election, councilmen were once again elected by place.

In their attempt to encourage industry to settle in College Station during the early 1980s, the council experienced what was probably the most serious conflict with a citizen group in the city's history. During a December 1980 Planning and Zoning Commission meeting, John Lawrence, a representative of an undisclosed firm, presented a request to rezone a fifty-four acre tract near the Raintree subdivision from single-family residential to planned industrial. The firm was considering the purchase of the land for the purpose of developing an industrial project. Lawrence described the industry as a light metal manufacturer listed among the top 500 companies in the nation. Developers of the proposed plant planned to employ 500 workers, including recreational facilities for employees, and allocate seventy-five percent of the property for landscaping. Lawrence also noted that the College Station Industrial Development Foundation would announce the identity of the firm at a future date.[45]

At the Planning and Zoning Commissions public hearings of Lawrence's request, several Raintree residents express their displeasure with the possible change. They emphatically stressed that the commission should not vote on the issue until they knew the identity of the industry. To placate the disgruntled citizens, Lawrence explained the company did not want to reveal its name until plans were finalized in order to avoid harassment from other firms and cities and that it was common for other large firms to adopt a similar philosophy. City Planner Albert Mayo also enumerated checks within the planned industrial zoning designation which allowed the city to regulate the type of

facility constructed. Although Commission Chairman Richard Maher sympathized with the residents' concerns, he believed a negative vote would seriously hamper industrial recruitment. With a vote of six to one, the commission approved the zoning change.[46]

Before the rezoning request was presented to the council for consideration, a group of Raintree residents met to discuss ways to block the change. The citizens warned of "extremely unfavorable consequences" and threatened a possible lawsuit if the motion passed. Since the rezoning measure contradicted the city's comprehensive plan, the residents argued that the plan would no longer be effective. City Planner Mayo explained that the master plan did not restrict the uses of the disputed property to residential, but that any new zoning designation must agree "with the character of the whole area." The group, however, felt the change would set a harmful precedent.[47]

During the January 8, 1981, council meeting, which drew an overflow crowd, many Raintree residents voiced strong opposition to the rezoning measure. They emphasized that "noise, traffic, and aesthetics" would prevent the industry from conforming to the character of the neighborhood. Even after hearing the citizens' objections, the council approved the proposal by a six to one vote. In an interview after the meeting, Mayor Gary Halter, a political science professor who ran unopposed in the 1980 municipal elections, revealed that most of the council members were already aware of the identity of the firm and expressed his belief that residents would be pleased with the industry. Councilman Robert Runnells, who had cast the dissenting vote, considered the secrecy aspect of the issue unnecessary and felt the decision would cause "an increased distrust in government."[48]

The Raintree group soon announced that they were forming a city-wide organization and would campaign for a recall election of all council members who approved the rezoning request. Mayor Halter believed such action would be detrimental for the community, and he pointed out the difficulty of obtaining the required signatures of forty percent of the qualified voters. Instead of a recall drive, Halter suggested that a better approach might be a referendum on whether or not zoning for the property should be industrial.[49]

On January 14, 1981, Westinghouse Electric Corporation disclosed that they had obtained an option to purchase the fifty-four-acre tract off the Highway 6 Bypass and were considering establishing a plant which would manufacture computer-related parts. Mayor Halter hoped the announcement from the respected firm would relieve the anxieties of Raintree residents, and Councilman Runnels admitted that the industry "has the potential for being a good community neighbor."[50] Within a week Westinghouse confirmed that they would buy the property. The company's spokesman, Tom Duncan, assured the neighboring residents that they would adhere to all environmental regulations, take aesthetics into account when designing the plant, and hopefully be an asset to the neighborhood.[51] Westinghouse finalized the purchase on March 4, 1981.

The Citizens for Responsible Government, the committee subsequently organized by Raintree residents, continued with their plans to block construction of the plant. Although they had a productive meeting with the mayor on January 16, the group decided to circulate a petition to force the city council to act on a referendum request. The residents believed that once they submitted the petition containing 300 signatures of qualified voters, the council had two legal options. Officials could call an

election and let the public determine the issue or they could repeal their earlier rezoning decision.[52]

To their dismay, members of the newly-formed organization learned that even if they presented a valid petition, the council would be under no legal obligation to call a referendum. College Station City Attorney Lowell Denton explained to the group that his study of several court cases and the state law verified that residents had no authority to enact or repeal zoning ordinances through referendums. The state specifically conferred authority for zoning matters to the council who in turn had to provide public hearings for citizen expression on the issue. Denton, who obtained the consensus of seven other municipal attorneys on his assessments, advised the group that holding an election would be futile since the results would be void. If they wanted to appeal the rezoning decision, they must file a suit in a court of law.[53]

Despite Denton's opinion, the Citizens for Responsible Government decided to proceed with their original course of action. On January 28, 1981, Chairman Robert Webb filed petitions containing 489 signatures with City Secretary Glenn Schroeder calling for repeal of the rezoning ordinance or the scheduling of a referendum. David Stasny, a Bryan attorney who represented some Raintree residents, believed the council was legally obligated to pursue one of the two choices presented in the petitions. College Station City Council set February 26, 1981, as the date for a public hearing on the issue.[54]

During the February public hearing, council members affirmed their previous decision, with an identical six to one vote, by denying both a repeal of and referendum on the rezoning ordinance. Agreeing with Denton's recommendations, the majority of the council viewed a referendum as a violation of state law, and they believed a repeal of the zoning designation could result in a lawsuit filed by Westinghouse which the city in all probability would lose.[55] The Raintree caucus immediately filed a suit against the College Station City Council. Represented by Stasny, they sought a court order to force the referendum. The group also vowed to be active in the upcoming municipal elections.[56]

Not all citizens shared the sentiments of the Citizens for Responsible Government. Another group, Citizens for Progress, was formed and advertised their support for the council and the industrial rezoning ordinance. Mayor Halter also received an informal petition with 600 signatures of residents which indicated approval of recent council actions.[57]

In order to prevent future friction, city officials discussed ways to smoothly assimilate industry into the community. Mayo suggested an industrial ordinance which would allow the council to fully review the compatibility of a proposed plant with the neighborhood and to enforce aesthetic conditions. The Planning and Zoning Commission agreed to research the land use concept which designated large sections of property in the city or just outside its limits for industrial, commercial, or residential development.[58] The council also decided to include a non-binding poll on the April 4, 1981, election ballot in order to canvass public opinion on how the city should approach industrial development.[59]

Although opposition groups created an atmosphere of controversy, the April 4th election revealed a mandate for the city government. Incumbent Councilmen Larry Ringer and Tony Jones were returned to their positions, and while Dr. Alvin Prause defeated incumbent Roy Kelly, Prause was not affiliated with the dissenting groups. The results of the informal poll showed that the majority of citizens concurred with the city's goal of industrial recruitment. They agreed that the council should financially support recruitment, and they believed officials should especially encourage the establishment of high technology industries and commercial facilities. Voters also approved the "flexible plan" which allowed zoning and land use changes that correspond with actual municipal development.[60]

The group of Raintree residents decided to end their fight against the rezoning measure in May 1981. The previous month Judge Bradley Smith ruled against their case because of insufficient evidence, and the contestants determined that an appeal would be too costly. Chairman Webb believed that the organization had achieved some accomplishments; he felt that the council would be more sensitive to the sentiments of residents in the future. Mayor Halter agreed that the situation could have been handled more diplomatically. The council might have spent additional time discussing the issue with Raintree residents before they voted on the ordinance.[61] With the conflict behind them and the results of the industry poll known, city officials now hoped to bring industry into the area without creating excessive discord.

Planning for the Future

City leaders worked to strengthen the framework of municipal operations during the 1970s and early 1980s so that College Station would become a self-reliant entity. Aware of the ramifications of undirected growth, officials decided to update the city's comprehensive plan. In late 1979, they began such a project with the purpose of evaluating College Station's current development and guiding its expansion into the next century. Within the same time period, the council invested in land for a proposed industrial park, an auspicious venture which promises to dynamically shape College Station's future goals, environment, and character.

Revision of the Pinnell 701 Plan commenced in October 1979 when the council appointed an advisory committee consisting of twelve citizens to study such municipal needs as land use programs, transportation, schools, industrial and commercial development, parks, and public service. Director of City Community Development James Callaway assigned the committee members to one of six designated areas in the city in order to gather citizens' viewpoints for the plan. The selected representatives scheduled several neighborhood meetings before city officials and the committee began formulating preliminary goals.[62]

Throughout 1980 the city planning department charted prospective land use maps, and officials and citizens compiled more that sixty long-range goals for "Plan 2000." In February 1981 City Planner Mayo presented a rough version of the goals to the Planning and Zoning Commission. Many of the objectives focused on establishing a harmonious land use arrangement. Mayo noted that citizens repeatedly stressed the necessity of avoiding strip zoning. Instead, they encouraged centralized commercial developments, industrial parks, and most importantly, the protection of single-family residential areas. Other goals included maintaining growth within the service capacity of the city, expanding the city staff to adequately serve the public, and analyzing some form of mass transit.[63] The council hired the consulting firms of Samual L. Wyse & Associates and Wayne W. Snyder & Associates in July 1981 to complete the preparation of the document.[64]

That same month College Station embarked on its most exciting municipal project. Hoping to utilize the much-discussed land use concept, the council approved on July 9, 1981 the purchase of 1,266 acres two miles south of the city limits for the location of future municipal facilities and an industrial park.[65] Originally, council members discussed buying 450 acres of that tract, which lay between Rock Prairie Road and Highway 6, for such new amenities as a sewer plant, cemetery, and warehouse, and for expansion of the city's landfill site located in the same vicinity. When presented with a favorable proposal that included 800 additional acres, the council agreed to accept the offer. They reasoned that the Industrial Foundation could buy or lease the remaining portion of the tract for industrial development.[66]

All the council members were enthusiastic about the impending acquisition. Councilwoman Patricia Boughton described it as "one of the best deals the city's made in a long, long time" while Councilman Larry Ringer termed it "an opportunity to purchase land that's vitally needed in the near future." Councilman James Dozier extolled the foresight of the transaction. "Very few cities," he explained, "have looked far ahead in areas of land purchase for city needs."[67] City Manager Bardell signed a $1.58 million contract with R. F. " Bob" Spearman, a local real estate developer, for the land on July 17, 1981, and within a week all accompanying details had been concluded.[68]

Richard Carter received a league of land for settlement from the government of Mexico in 1831, and built his home on Carter Creek in October of that year, thus becoming "College Station's" first resident. His statue is located in the Richard Carter Park along the east by-pass.

COURTESY DEPARTMENT OF PARKS AND RECREATION

At the turn of the century the Shiloh Community, now encompassed within the city limits, was a farm community which boasted a one-room school. Pictured, left to right (back row) are: Liddie Hrdlicka, Prusa Barta, Emma Stasney, Fannie Blazek, Victoria Kapchinsky, Josie Stasny, John Blazek, Janie Stasny, Ed Boriskie, Albina Boriskie, Sophie Kapchinsky, John Boriskie; (second row) Stella Hrdlicka, Mary Hedvica, Frank Boriskie, Mary Stasny, Mary Barak, Annie Blazek, Nora Elbrick, Marky Kulak, Victoria Domink, Albina Blazek, Mary Hrdlicka, Frank Kulak, John Holik; (front row) John Kulak, Tom Holik, Joe Hrdlicka, Leon Stasny, Louis Domenik, Frank Dominik, Leon Boriskie, Lawrence Stasny, Frank Kulak. The teacher is John Stasny.

COURTESY MRS. JANIE KRENEK

Boyett's Store about 1915. The Boyett family played a major role in the development of the city's commercial district on the North side of the Campus.

COURTESY TEXAS A&M UNIVERSITY ARCHIVES

Students board the interurban for Bryan. A gasoline trolley began operation in 1908. It converted to electricity in 1915, and was replaced by a bus line in 1923.

COURTESY TEXAS A&M UNIVERSITY ARCHIVES

The Shirley Hotel was built on the A&M Campus in 1906 by private subscriptions from faculty to help solve the housing shortage. The Shirley was named for the daughter of professor John A. Lomax. It was the inn for visitors, a temporary quarters for faculty families awaiting regular housing, and a residence hotel for bachelor professors. Mrs. Asa J. Neff operated the dining room.

COURTESY TEXAS A&M UNIVERSITY ARCHIVES

North Gate about 1920 provided the community its first "commercial strip shopping center." The United States Post Office in on the left.

COURTESY TEXAS A&M UNIVERSITY ARCHIVES

The "College" and the "Station" dominate the landscape in this 1925 aerial view of the A&M College. Faculty and staff lived on campus in Campus-owned housing (lower left and right), or commuted to Bryan, some four unpaved miles away.

COURTEST FORMER STUDENTS ASSOCIATION

Luke Patranella and Charles Opersteny operated a grocery in the Boyett's building from 1925-1929, and in the latter year Patranella opened a grocery in the College Station Village (East Gate), which he operated until his death in 1946.

COURTESY MRS. ELSIE SAUER

The home above is one of College Station's first off-campus residences located across "Dexter Lake" on what is now West Dexter Stree. The home in the 1980s is the property of Doc Burk.

COURTESY BILL LANCASTER

Although an Independent School District was organized as early as 1909, public educated laced a real tax based until the incorporation of the City in 1938. This building was constructed on campus in 1920, and served school-aged children until the construction of the "new" A&M Consolidated School on the corner of Jersey and Holik in 1940.

COURTESY TEXAS A&M UNIVERSITY ARCHIVES

The first map of the City of College Station (1939) shows residential areas south of the Texas A&M University Campus along Jersey and the Wellborn Road, "Boyett's Addition" near Northgate, and College Hills estates east of the campus along Highway 6.

COURTESY CITY OF COLLEGE STATION

The first College Station City Council, 1938-1939. From left to right, John S. Hopper, City Marshall; Letcher P. Gabbard, George B. Wilcox, John H. Binney, Ernest Langford, Alva Mitchell, Luther G. Jones.
COURTESY TEXAS A&M UNIVERSITY ARCHIVES

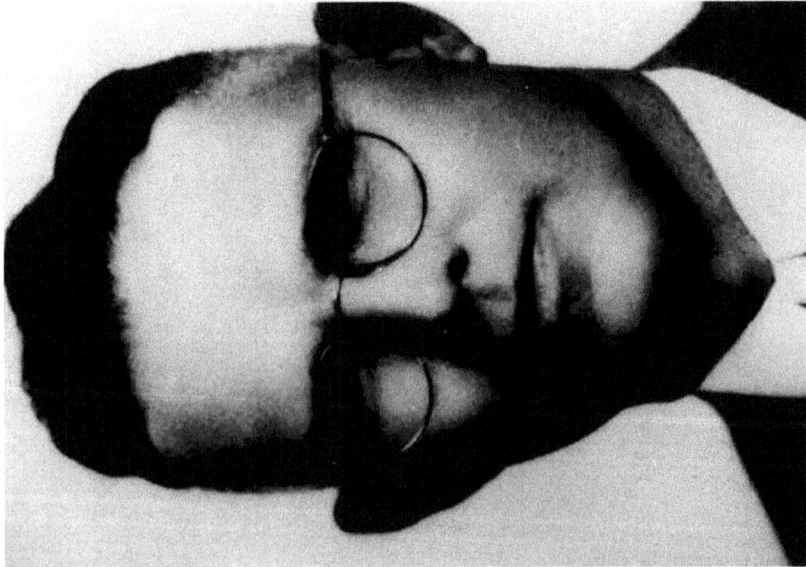

Frank G. Anderson
College Station Mayor 1940-1949

COURTESY
CITY OF COLLEGE STATION

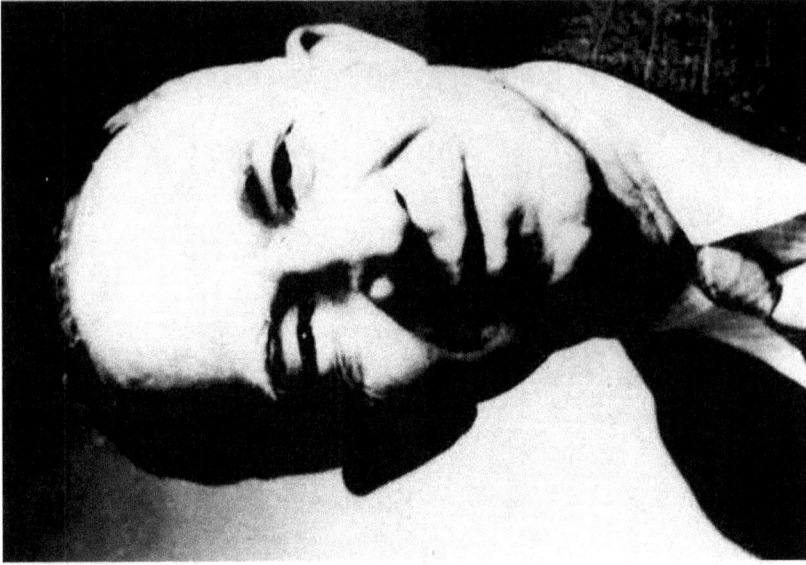

John H. Binney
College Station Mayor 1939-1940

COURTESY
CITY OF COLLEGE STATION

This aerial view of Texas A&M University and College Station taken about 1946 indicates little change in the residential and commercial areas of the City since its incorporation in 1938.

COURTESY CITY OF COLLEGE STATION

This composite view shows the development of the three business districts surrounding the College as of 1948. Top – North Gate; Middle – East Gate; Bottom – Southside.

COURTESY TEXAS A&M UNIVERSITY ARCHIVES

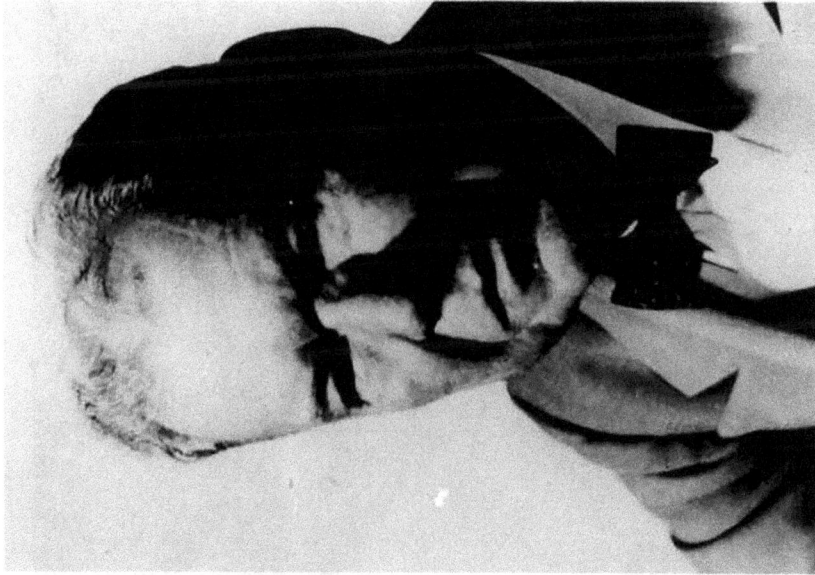

David A. Anderson
College Station Mayor 1966-1971
COURTESY
CITY OF COLLEGE STATION

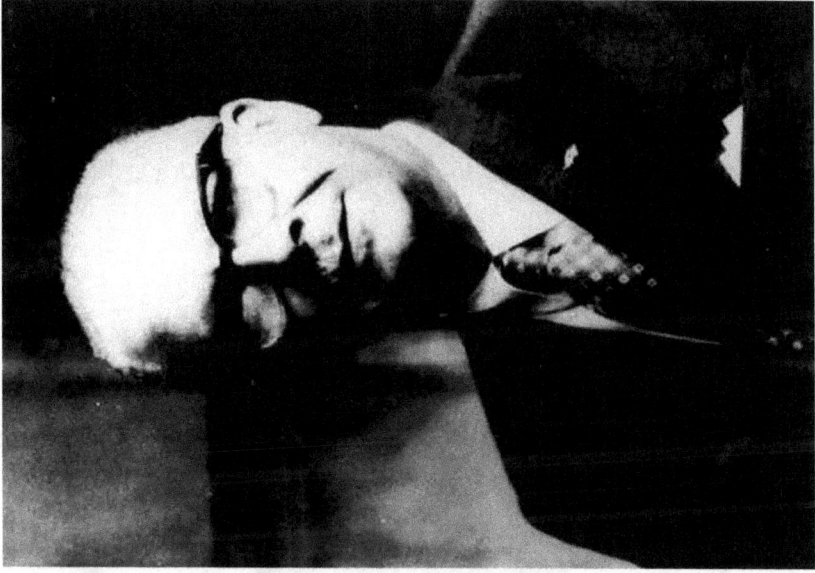

Ernest Langford
College Station Mayor 1942-1946
COURTESY
CITY OF COLLEGE STATION

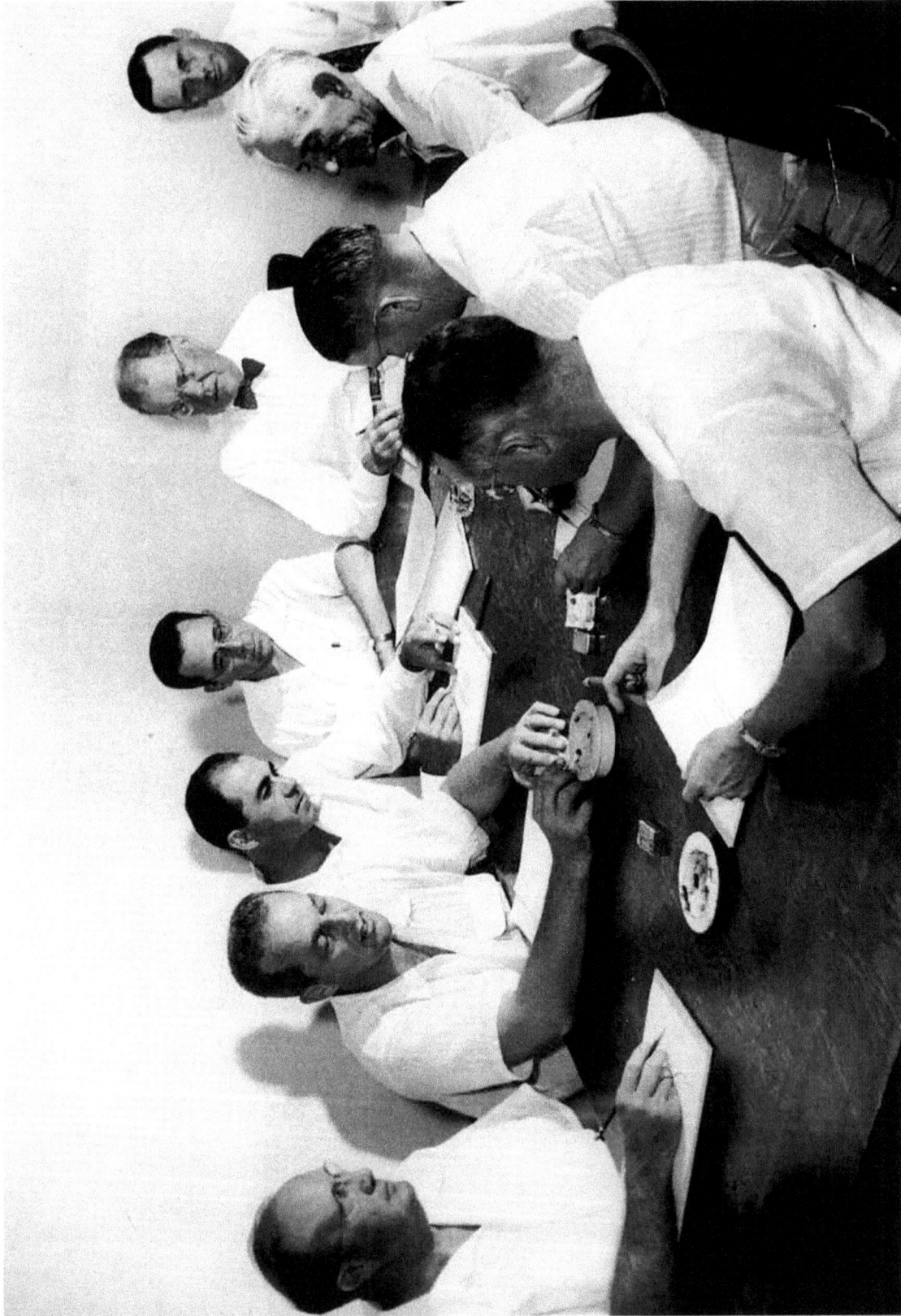

The 1952 City Council in a planning meeting. Left to right are: J. Wheeler Barger, Bill Fitch, Marion Pugh, Joe Sorrels, Mayor Ernest Langford, Howard Badgett, Harry Boyer, N.M. McGinnis, and City Manger Ran Boswell.
COURTESY CITY OF COLLEGE STATION

City Mangers Ran Boswell (left) 1952-1974 and North Bardell (right) 1974-1986, managed the business affairs of the City through most of its first fifty years.
COURTESY *THE EAGLE*

The City Council in January 1967, at the beginning of a period of unparalleled growth and expansion, included, standing, left to right: A.L. Rosprin, City Manager Ran Boswell, Robert R. Rhodes, Dr. O.M. Holt, Attorney Don Dillon, and Secretary C.F. Richardson. Seated: A.P. Boyett, Mayor D.A. Anderson, B.J. Cooley, and Homer B. Adams.

COURTESY CITY OF COLLEGE STATION

W.A. Tarrow served as a teacher and principal in the College Station schools (Lincoln High School and College Station Elementary) for over twenty years. He is pictured here with students in Mrs. Brown's sixth grade: (Front row, left to right) Keith Boutain, Jimmy Bohanan, Shelia Taylor, Delphine Barron, Kathy Dawson (Back row, left to right) Principal W.A. Tarrow, Kennard Roy, Charles Merchant, Michael Lenz, Hebree Searcy, Richard Groot, Mary Brown. Tarrow helped organized and served as preside of Community House, a day care and social services organization begun with private donations and volunteers in 1953. He received the Lane Bryant Award for distinguished community service, presented at the Plaza Hotel in New York City in 1966.

COURTESY EDNA TARROW AND HELEN SIMPSON

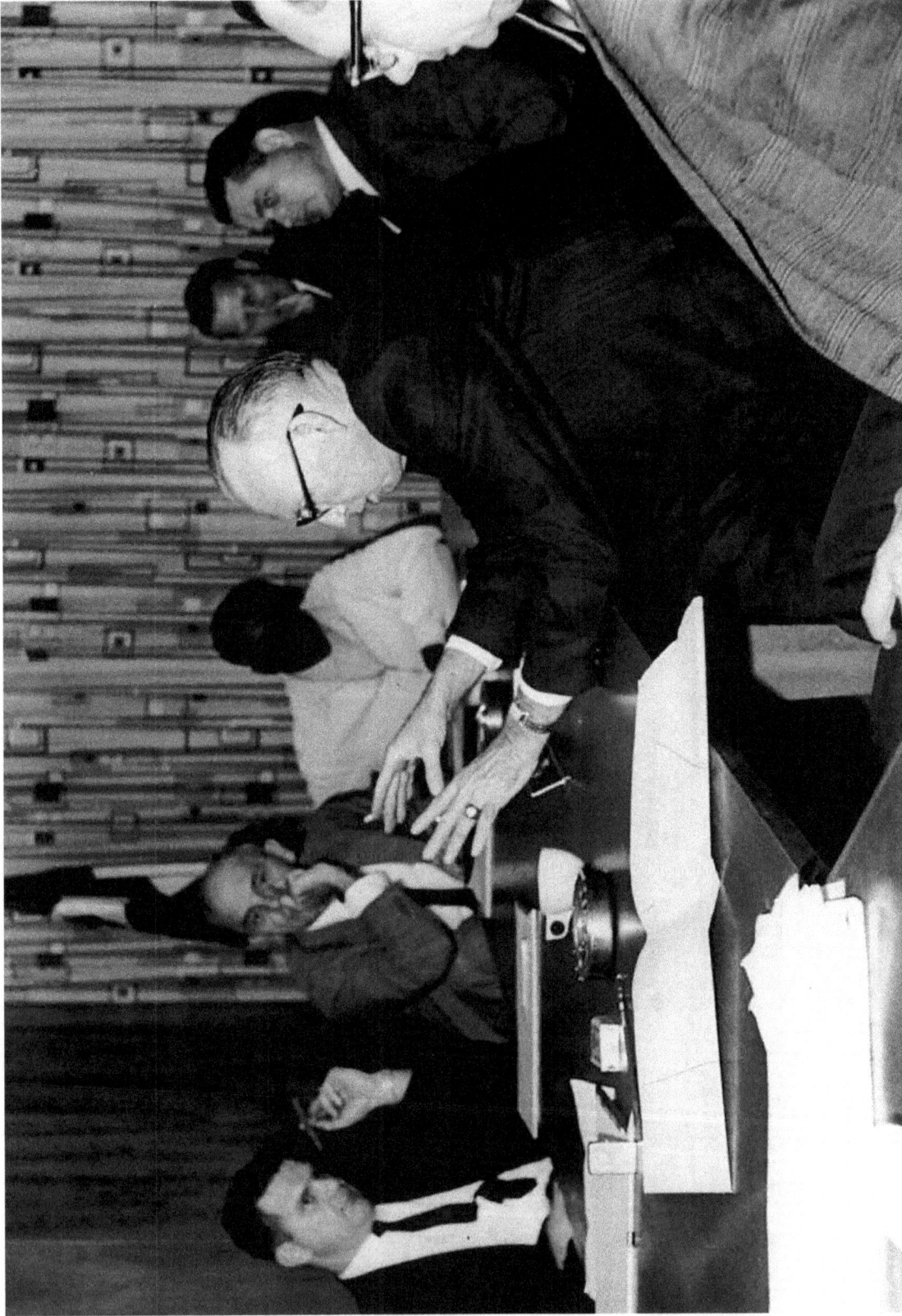

The College Station Planning and Zoning Commission meets with Mayor O.M. Holt to discuss expansion plans. Present are (left to right) Dennis Goenring, Everett Janne, Tommy Preston, Bill Smith, Ed Cooper, Mayor Holt, and City Manager Ran Boswell.

COURTESY CITY OF COLLEGE STATION

Lorence Bravanec
College Station Mayor 1976-1979

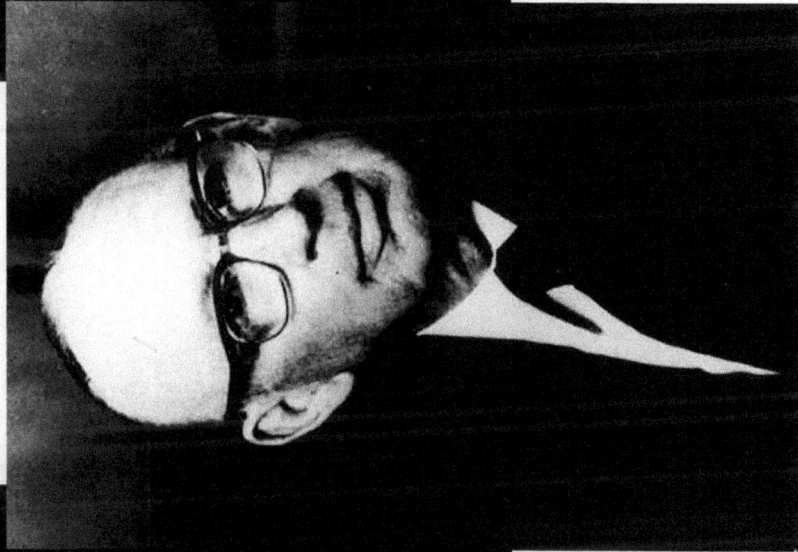

Oris M. Holt
College Station Mayor 1974-1976

James B. "Dick" Hervey
College Station Mayor 1971-1974

The expansion of Jersey Street in 1968 provided better access to the A&M Campus. This view is looking west from Anderson Street.

COURTESY CITY OF COLLEGE STATION

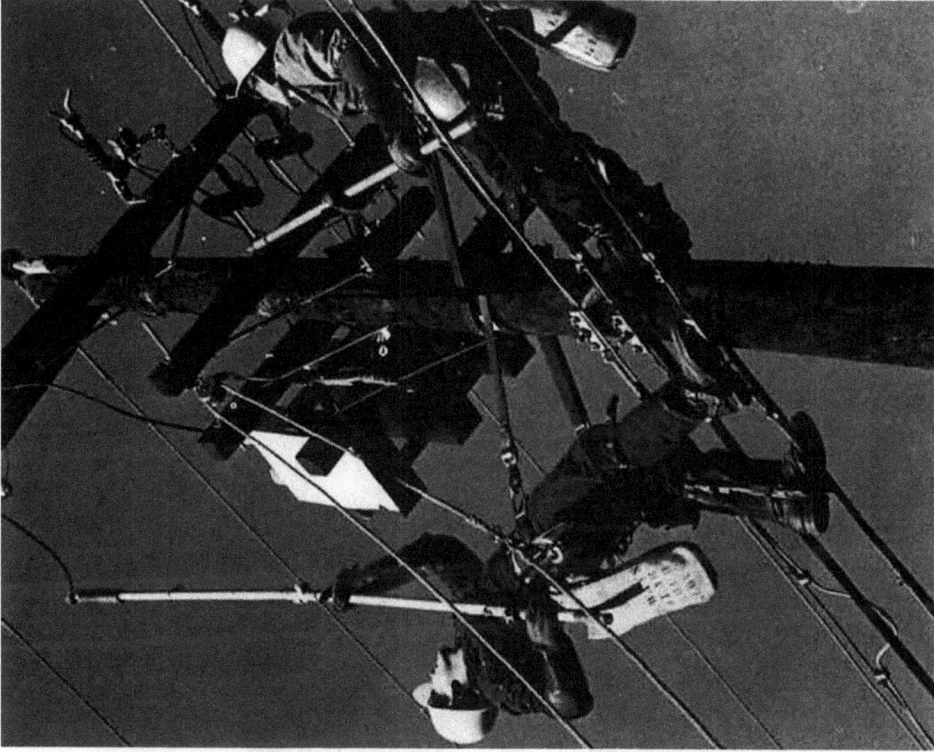

Rapid city growth in the 1970s kept utilities and power crews occupied constantly. For many years the City received utility services and fire protection from Texas A&M University or Bryan.
COURTESY CITY OF COLLEGE STATION

Completion of the east by-pass in the 1970s eased the traffic problems on Highway 6, which had become the main commercial artery for Bryan and College Station in the 1950s and 1960s.

COURTESY CITY OF COLLEGE STATION

90

This scene from Gabbard Park suggests the considerable investment in community parks and recreational facilities by the people of College Station, who have a commitment to a quality living environment.

COURTESY DEPARTMENT OF PARKS AND RECREATION

"Action" and "activity" are bywords of the College Station community where two-thirds of the population, when Texas A&M University's 40,000 students are included, are under the age of twenty-one.
COURTESY DEPARTMENT OF PARKS AND RECREATION

Little League action about 1975 at Wayne Smith Park. New park and field developments in the 1980 have caused the retirement and razing of the old ball field at Wayne Smith, which provided almost three decades of play for College Station youth.
COURTESY CITY OF COLLEGE STATION

Community Education Programs for youth and adults offer athletics of all kinds, and include instructional programs, exercise, health care, pottery, weaving, computers and languages, among the many options.
COURTESY DEPARTMENT OF PARKS AND RECREATION

The "World Headquarters" of the College Station Department of Recreation and Parks in Central Park. COURTESY DEPARTMENT OF PARKS AND RECREATION

The "Second" City Hall, completed in 1970.

COURTESY CITY OF COLLEGE STATION

The City Hall Annex, completed in 1984, blends with the City Hall to provide a modern and comfortable municipal complex.

COURTESY CITY OF COLLEGE STATION

Texas Street or Highway 6 is the major thoroughfare for College Station and Bryan. On the horizon to the left is the Oceanography Building on the Texas A&M University Campus, and in the center is the Ramada Inn.

Larry Ringer
College Station Mayor 1986-

Gary Halter
College Station Mayor 1980-1986

This winter snow scene is on the pond at Central Park, taken in 1986.
COURTESY DEPARTMENT OF PARKS AND RECREATION

Chapter I

1. Rupert N. Richardson, Ernest Wallace, and Adrian Anderson, *Texas: The Lone Star State*, 3rd ed. (Engelwood Cliffs, New Jersey: Prentice-Hall, Inc., 1970), p. 9.
2. Joseph Milton Nance, *The Early History of Bryan and the Surrounding Area* (Bryan, Texas: Hood's Brigade — Bryan Centennial Committee, 1962.) p. 1.
3. *Ibid.*
4. *Ibid.*
5. T.R. Fehrenbach, *Lone Star: A History of Texas and the Texans* (New York: The Dial Press, 1968), pp. 90 – 91.
6. Kate Efnor, "Historical Sketch of Brazos County, Texas," *American Sketch Book* 4 (1879), p. 237.
7. Shawn Carlson, *College Station's First Settler* (College Station, Texas: Arts Council of Brazos Valley, [n.d.]), p. 4.
8. Nance, *Early History of Bryan*, p. 2.
9. Efnor, "Historical Sketch," p. 237.
10. Elmer Grady Marshall, "The History of Brazos County, Texas" (M.A. thesis, University of Texas at Austin, 1937), p. 28.
11. Efnor, "Historical Sketch," p. 242.
12. *Ibid.*
13. Nance, *Early History of Bryan*, p. 1.
14. Marshall, "History of Brazos County," p. 8.
15. *Brazos County Historical Tour*, Compiled by students of Bryan High School under the direction of Mrs. Charlene Ragsdale (Bryan, Texas: Wallace Printing Co., 1976), p. 5.
16. Efnor, "Historical Sketch," pp. 239 – 240.
17. Shawn Carlson, "The Economic Development of an East Central Texas Rancher 1931 – 1878," paper presented at the 53rd meeting of the Texas Archeological Society, College Station, Texas, October 1982, pp. 3 – 4.
18. *Ibid.*
19. Nance, *Early History of Bryan*, p. 13.
20. *Ibid.*, p. 27.
21. *Ibid.*
22. Carlson, "Economic Development," pp. 4 – 5.
23. Marshall, "History of Brazos County," p. 106.
24. Henry C. Dethloff, *A Centennial History of Texas A&M University*, 2 vols. (College Station, Texas: Texas A&M University Press, 1975), I, pp. 16 – 17.
25. Marshall, "History of Brazos County," p. 119 – 121.
26. Ernest Langford, *Getting the College Under Way* (College Station, Texas: University Library, 1970), pp. 1 – 5.
27. C.W. Crawford and others, *One Hundred Years of Engineering at Texas A&M 1876 1976* (College Station, Texas: By the Author, 1976), p. 3.
28. Dethloff, *Centennial History of Texas A&M*, I, pp. 18, 20 – 21.
29. *Ibid.*, I, p. 3.
30. *Ibid.*, I, p. 19.

31. Clarence Ousley, *History of the Agricultural and Mechanical College of Texas* (College Station, Texas: Agricultural and Mechanical College of Texas, 1935), pp. 40 – 41.
32. Crawford, *One Hundred Years of Engineering*, p. 4.
33. Joseph M. Nance, foreword to Henry C. Dethloff, *A Centennial History of Texas A&M University*, 2 vols. (College Station, Texas: Texas A&M University Press, 1975), I, p. xi.
34. Crawford, *One Hundred Years of Engineering*, p. 4.
35. Langford, *Getting the College Under Way*, p. 55.
36. Dethloff, *Centennial History of Texas A&M*, I, p. 44.
37. *Ibid.*, I, p. 46.
38. Jane Mills Smith, "CS Recent Community," *The Eagle*, June 24, 1979, in College Station Publicity Notebook, vol. 19, p. 142.
39. *Ibid.*
40. Robert Franklin Smith, "A Brief Sketch of the Agricultural and Mechanical College of Texas," 1914, in Harvey Mitchell File, Texas A&M University Archives, College Station, Texas.
41. David Brooks Cofer, ed., *Early History of Texas A&M College through Letters and Papers* (College Station, Texas: Association of Former Students, 1952), pp. 82 – 84.
42. Dethloff, *Centennial History of Texas A&M*, I, pp. 158, 166.
43. *Ibid.*, I, p. 181.
44. Marshall, "History of Brazos County," p. 108.
45. James L. Rock and W. I. Smith, *South and Western Texas Guide for 1878* (St. Louis, Missouri: A. H. Granger, 1878), p. 53.
46. Estelle Hudson and Henry R. Maresh, *Czech Pioneers of the Southwest*, (Dallas, Texas: South-West Press, Inc., 1934), p. 38.
47. Interview with Herman Krenek, April 28, 1983.
48. *Ibid.*
49. *Ibid.*
50. *Ibid.*
51. *Ibid.*
52. *Ibid.*
53. *Ibid.*
54. *Brazos County Historical Tour*, p. 9.
55. Rock and Smith, *Texas Guide for 1878*, p. 53.
56. Interview with Krenek.
57. *Ibid.*
58. *Ibid.*
59. *Ibid.*
60. City of College Station, Minutes of the Meeting of City Council, vol. 3, October 15, 1947, p. 242.
61. Agricultural and Mechanical College of Texas, *Annual Catalog, 1900* (College Station, Texas: Agricultural and Mechanical College of Texas, 1900), p. 82.
62. Ernest Langford, *Remembrance of Things Past* (College Station, Texas: By the Author, 1975), p. 156.
63. Dethloff, *Centennial History of Texas A&M*, I, p. 198.

64. David Brooks Cofer, *Fragments of Early History of Texas A&M College* (College Station, Texas: Association of Former Students, 1953), p. 36.
65. Dethloff, *Centennial History of Texas A&M*, I, p. 226.
66. *Ibid.*, I, pp. 228 – 229.
67. Cofer, ed., *Letters and Papers*, p. 83.
68. Cofer, *Fragments*, p. 10.
69. Dethloff, *Centennial History of Texas A&M*, I, p. 160.
70. Cofer, *Fragments*, p. 10.
71. *Ibid.*
72. George Sessions Perry, *The Story of Texas A&M* (New York: McGraw-Hill Book Co., 1951), p. 81.
73. *Ibid.*
74. Dethloff, *Centennial History of Texas A&M*, II, p. 407.
75. Interview with C.A. Bonnen, March 25, 1983.
76. Langford, *Remembrance*, p. 120.
77. Tad Moses, "Your City — Fifth of a Series," *Battalion*, July 12, 1945, in College Station Publicity Notebook, vol. 1, p. 69.
78. *Ibid.*
79. Interview with Hershel Burgess, 16 March 1983.
80. *Ibid.*
81. *Ibid.*

Chapter II

1. Agricultural and Mechanical College of Texas, *The Longhorn, 1938* (College Station, Texas: Agricultural and Mechanical College of Texas, 1938); Interview with J.O. White, July 11, 1983.
2. Henry C. Dethloff, *A Centennial History of Texas A&M University*, 2 vols. (College Station, Texas: Texas A&M University Press, 1975), II, p. 424.
3. "Your City," *Battalion*, undated clipping, in College Station Publicity Notebook, vol. 1, p. 65.
4. Tad Moses, "Your City," *Battalion*, undated clipping, in College Station Publicity Notebook, vol. 1, p. 66.
5. "Your City," undated clipping, vol. 1, p. 65.
6. *Ibid.*
7. Elmer Grady Marshall, "The History of Brazos County, Texas" (M.A. thesis, University of Texas at Austin, 1937), p. 213.
8. Interview with Hershel Burgess, March 16, 1983; Interview with C.A. Bonnen, March 25, 1983.
9. Moses, "Your City," vol. 1, p. 66.
10. Petition to the Board of Directors, A. and M. College, through the President of the College, College Station, Texas, March 4, 1938, p. 1.
11. *Ibid.*, pp. 3 – 4.
12. *Ibid.*, pp. 2 – 4.
13. *Ibid.*, p. 4.
14. *Ibid.*

15. "Election on Proposal Is to be Asked," *Bryan Eagle*, March 23, 1938, in College Station Publicity Notebook, vol. 1, p. 1.
16. Revised Civil Statutes of the State of Texas (1925), Title 28, pp. 289, 340.
17. Petition to the County Judge of Brazos County, Texas from Residents of the Unincorporated Town of College Station, College Station, Texas, June 2, 1938, p. 1.
18. "College Station Property Holders Will Vote Oct. 19," *Bryan Eagle*, October 8, 1938, in College Station Publicity Notebook, vol. 1, p. 5.
19. Interview with Charles Crawford, March 24, 1983.
20. Interview with Bonnen.
21. "College Area Citizens for Municipality," *Bryan Eagle*, October 20, 1938, in College Station Publicity Notebook, vol. 1, p. 7.
22. "Election of City Officials Due Nov. 28," *Battalion*, November 4, 1938.
23. "Officials for City Nominated," *Battalion*, November 15, 1938.
24. "College Station Names Mayor and Five Alderman," *Houston Post*, November 30, 1938, in College Station Publicity Notebook, vol. 1, p. 28.
25. "Ruling to be Sought as to Eligibility," *Bryan Eagle*, December 19, 1938, in College Station Publicity Notebook, vol. 1, p. 35.
26. Robert Stewart, "Mayor Langford Views Birth, Growth of Town," *Bryan Daily Eagle*, August 2, 1964, in College Station Publicity Notebook, vol. 5, p. 111.
27. "College Station Goes into Municipal Rule," *Waco Tribune-Herald*, February 26, 1939, in College Station Publicity Notebook, vol. 1, p. 43.
28. City of College Station, Minutes of Meeting of City Council, vol 1, March 9, 1939 and March 23, 1939, pp. 3, 7.
29. *Ibid.*, vol. 1, February 25, 1939, February 27, 1939, March 6, 1939 and March 9, 1939, pp. 1 – 5.
30. *Ibid.*, vol. 1, April 5, 1939 and April 12, 1939, pp. 9 – 11.
31. *Ibid.*, vol. 1, April 20, 1939 and May 18, 1939, pp. 13, 16.
32. City of College Station, Ordinances, vol. 1, March 16, 1939 and April 20, 1939, pp. 4, 13 – 14.
33. Minutes, vol. 1, June 8, 1939, p. 19.
34. Ordinances, vol. 1, April 12, 1939, p. 11.
35. "City Tax Situation," *Battalion*, October 1939, in College Station Publicity Notebook, vol. 1, p. 62.
36. Minutes, vol. 1, June 8, 1939 and July 6, 1939, pp. 19 – 22.
37. *Ibid.*, vol. 1, March 30, 1939, September 18, 1939 and November 17, 1939, pp. 8, 27, 35.
38. *Ibid.*, vol. 1, September 18, 1939, p. 27.
39. Ordinances, vol. 1, September 28, 1939, p. 37.
40. Minutes, vol. 1, February 6, 1940 and February 29, 1940, pp. 45, 47.
41. Ordinances, vol. 1, February 15, 1940 and February 29, 1940, pp. 94, 95.
42. Minutes, vol. 1, September 5, 1940 and October 28, 1940, pp. 67, 71.
43. Interview with Luther G. Jones, March 25, 1983.
44. Creation of Agricultural and Mechanical College Independent School District, S. B. No 70, in City of College Station Files, Texas A&M University Archives, College Station, Texas.

Chapter III

1. Interview with David A. Anderson, September 22, 1983.
2. Robert Stewart, "Mayor Langford Views Birth, Growth of Town," *Bryan Daily Eagle*, August 2, 1964, in College Station Publicity Notebook, vol. 5, p. 111.
3. Ernest Langford, *Remembrance of Things Past* (College Station, Texas: By the Author, 1975), pp. 18, 45.
4. Stewart, "Mayor Langford," vol. 5, p. 111.
5. Langford, *Remembrance*, pp. 95 – 119.
6. *Ibid.*, pp. 122, 128 – 129.
7. Donald D. Burchard, "Profile: Ernest Langford," *Brazos Valley Review*, August 31, 1961, in College Station Publicity Notebook, vol. 4, p. 42.
8. City of College Station, Minutes of Meeting of City Council, vol. 2, January 28, 1943, p. 123.
9. David R. Goldfield and Blaine A. Brownell, *Urban America: From Downtown to No Town* (Boston, Mass.: Houghton Mifflin Company, 1979), p. 359.
10. Agricultural and Mechanical College of Texas, *Annual Catalog, 1926* (College Station, Texas: Agricultural and Mechanical College of Texas, 1926).
11. City of College Station, Ordinances, vol. 1, October 22, 1942, pp. 161 – 162.
12. Minutes, vol. 2, November 30, 1942, p. 121.
13. "College Station Adopts Manager Plan," *Texas Municipalities* 31 (May 1944), p. 97.
14. City of College Station, Minutes of Meeting of City Council, vol. 3, February 20, 1947, July 6, 1948 and June 12, 1950, pp. 225, 263, 334.
15. Minutes, vol. 2, September 13, 1945, p. 172.
16. "Big Crowd Urged for Bond Meeting at College Station," unidentified newspaper clipping, December 19, 1950, in College College Station Publicity Notebook, vol. 1, p. 206.
17. George Charlton, "City Makes Rapid Growth in Short 12 Year History," unidentified newspaper clipping, undated, in College Station Publicity Notebook, vol. 1, p. 171.
18. "College Station City Operations," unidentified newspaper clipping, undated, in College Station Publicity Notebook, vol. 1, p. 89.
19. "College Station's City Council Will Hold Open House," unidentified newspaper clipping, December 13, 1950, in College Station Publicity Notebook, vol. 1, p. 206.
20. Minutes, vol. 3, November 14, 1949, p. 296.
21. "College Station City Unusual Community," *The Bryan News*, February 14, 1950, in College Station Publicity Notebook, vol. 1, p. 177.
22. "Steen Announces Platform for Mayor's Race; Adopts Slogan, 'Build College Station Now,'" *Battalion*, March 27, 1946, in College Station Publicity Notebook, vol. 1, p. 119.
23. "City Out-Grabs Bryan for Land," *Battalion*, April 13, 1951, in College Station Publicity Notebook, vol. 2, p. 26.
24. Institute of Public Affairs, *Texas Council-Manager Charters* (Austin, Texas: The University of Texas, 1961), p. 1.

45. W.L. Hughes, "Your City — Sixth of a Series," *Battalion*, July 19, 1945, in College Station Publicity Notebook, vol. 1, p. 70.
46. "Early School Districts Traced," *Eagle*, June 24, 1979, in College Station Publicity Notebook, vol. 19, p. 142.
47. Hughes, "Your City — Sixth of a Series," p. 70.
48. *Ibid.*
49. *Ibid.*
50. W.L. Hughes, "Your City — Seventh of a Series," *Battalion*, July 26, 1945, in College Station Publicity Notebook, vol. 1, p. 71.
51. W.L. Hughes, "Your City — Eighth of a Series," *Battalion*, August 2, 1945, in College Station Publicity Notebook, vol. 1, p. 72.
52. W.D. Bunting, "Your City — Ninth of a Series," *Battalion*, August 2, 1945, in College Station Publicity Notebook, vol. 1, p. 73.
53. "Incorporation Is Discussed at A. and M. Meeting," *Bryan Eagle*, October 18, 1938, in College Station Publicity Notebook, vol. 1, p. 6.
54. Bunting, "Your City," vol. 1, p. 73.
55. Interview with Bonnen.
56. City of College Station, Community Center: Grand Opening, College Station, Texas, June 13, 1982. [Typescript.]
57. John Mitchell, *et al.*, March 13, 1939, to Mr. E.E. Vezey, Chairman of Board of Trustees, A. and M. Consolidated School, in City Hall Miscellaneous Files, College Station, Texas.
58. S.B. Zisman, "Community Plans its Schools," *American School and University* 13 (1941), pp. 28 – 36.
59. Bunting, "Your City," vol. 1, p. 73.
60. Interview with Jones.
61. Bunting, "Your City," vol. 1, p. 73.
62. Bill Clarkson, "College Station Is Fastest Growing City for its Size in State of Texas," unidentified newspaper clipping, undated, in College Station Publicity Notebook, vol. 1, p. 64.
63. Interview with Crawford.
64. Clarkson, "College Station," vol. 1, p. 64.
65. Interview with Burgess.
66. "Incorporation of College Station Has Resulted in Greater Expansion and Passage of Needed Regulations," *Battalion*, November 18, 1939.
67. Ordinances, vol. 1, July 6, 1989, p. 23.
68. *Ibid.*, vol. 1, January 22, 1940, pp. 54 – 88.
69. Minutes, vol. 1, December 7, 1939, p. 37.
70. Ordinances, vol. 1, May 25, 1939, p. 21.
71. Minutes, vol. 1, February 15, 1940, p. 46.
72. Interview with Frank G. Anderson, March 23, 1983.
73. *Ibid.*
74. *Ibid.*
75. Minutes, vol. 1, April 2, 1940, p. 52.
76. Interview with Anderson.
77. *Ibid.*
78. Minutes, vol. 1, April 17, 1941, p. 87.
79. Interview with Anderson.

25. Minutes, vol. 3, June 12, 1950, p. 334.

26. Joel Austin, "Committee Discusses Charter," *Battalion*, April 5, 1951, in College Station Publicity Notebook, vol. 2, p. 34.

27. The Charter of the City of College Station, City Charters and Amendments, Book 13, in Texas State Archives, Austin, Texas, pp. 137 – 144.

28. *Ibid*, p. 139.

29. *Ibid*, pp. 153 – 155.

30. City of College Station, Minutes of City Council, vol. 4, January 9, 1952, p. 443.

31. Jon Kinslow, "Boswell Serving Third Year Here," *Battalion*, February 24, 1955, in College Station Publicity Notebook, vol. 2, p. 88.

32. Minutes, vol. 3, December 17, 1946 and January 9, 1951, pp. 206, 372; Minutes, vol. 4, December 2, 1954, p. 524.

33. Minutes, vol. 3, September 12, 1946, p. 194.

34. Joel Austin, "Electricity Story, Past Views Told," *Battalion*, February 23, 1951, in College Station Publicity Notebook, vol. 2, p. 18.

35. *Ibid*.

36. "CS Hands Bryan $38,109 Check for REA Lines," *Battalion*, March 31, 1951, in College Station Publicity Notebook, vol. 2, p. 21.

37. Minutes, vol. 3, April 11, 1949, p. 280.

38. *Ibid*, vol. 3, January 9, 1951, p. 373.

39. "Bond Issue Approved by College Station Voters 431 – 20," *Battalion*, December 2, 1954, in College Station Publicity Notebook, vol. 2, p. 75.

40. Minutes, vol. 4, August 15, 1955 and May 28, 1956, pp. 545, 567.

41. Bill Cobble, "Your Fire Department Offers Best for Less," *Battalion*, June 9, 1956, in College Station Publicity Notebook, vol. 2, p. 57.

42. "Little Action in City Council," *Battalion*, March 26, 1957, in College Station Publicity Notebook, vol. 2, p. 182; "College Station Makes Fire Insurance Study," *Bryan Daily Eagle*, August 23, 1960 and "Changes Urged by State Man," *Bryan Daily Eagle*, August 23, 1960, in College Station Publicity Notebook, vol. 3, pp. 151, 152.

43. "City Budget Discussed at Hearing Last Night," unidentified newspaper clipping, August 5, 1949, in College Station Publicity Notebook, vol. 1, p. 105.

44. "City Council Assigns New Water Contracts," *Battalion*, November 27, 1956, in College Station Publicity Notebook, vol. 2, p. 160.

45. "Charter Is Granted for College Station Bank; Location is Undetermined," *Battalion*, November 8, 1945, in College Station Publicity Notebook, vol. 1, p. 82.

46. Interview with Hershel Burgess, March 16, 1983.

47. *Ibid*.

48. Minutes, vol. 3, June 8, 1946 and December 12, 1946, pp. 188, 204.

49. City of College Station, A Condensed History of College Station Cemetery, College Station, October 27, 1966, pp. 1 – 2. [Typescript.]

50. Interview with C.A. Bonnen, March 25, 1983.

51. Otto Kunze, "City Council Takes Action for Library," *Battalion*, August 17, 1949, in College Station Publicity Notebook, vol. 1, p. 160.

52. Minutes, vol. 3, July 15, 1947, p. 234.

53. Jon Kinslow, "Election to Decide Recreation Tax Increase," *Battalion*, January 29, 1953, in College Station Publicity Notebook, vol. 2, p. 50.

54. Minutes, vol. 4, April 28, 1953, p. 479.

55. City of College Station, Ordinances, vol. 3, January 30, 1953, p. 438.

56. "New Street Plan Unveiled at Meeting," *Bryan Daily Eagle*, February 25, 1958, in College Station Publicity Notebook, vol. 3, p. 11.

57. "CS Plant Nursery Completed Monday," *Battalion*, March 12, 1958, in College Station Publicity Notebook, vol. 3, p. 17.

58. Gayle McNutt, "Council Making Bid for Better Streets," *Battalion*, November 26, 1957, in College Station Publicity Notebook, vol. 2, p. 207.

59. *Ibid*.

60. "College Station Property Owners Faced with Dilemma," *Bryan Daily Eagle*, January 19, 1958, in College Station Publicity Notebook, vol. 3, p. 1.

61. "City Council Announces Policy on Street Repair, New Building," *Battalion*, November 12, 1958, in College Station Publicity Notebook, vol. 3, p. 61.

62. Dave Stoker, "Petition for Street Bond Vote Presented to CS City Council," *Battalion*, November 25, 1958, in College Station Publicity Notebook, vol. 3, p. 67.

63. "New Street Plan Unveiled," vol. 3, p. 11.

64. "Street Bond Vote Set by CS Council," *Bryan Daily Eagle*, January 27, 1959, in College Station Publicity Notebook, vol. 3, p. 72.

65. Johnny Johnson, "Heavy Vote Blasts Street Bond Issue," *Battalion*, February 18, 1959, in College Station Publicity Notebook, vol. 3, p. 85.

66. "Civic Leaders Plan Discussion of Expansion," *Battalion*, February 19, 1957, in College Station Publicity Notebook, vol. 2, p. 169.

67. Gayle McNutt, "Brazos County Planners Hear Expansion Plan," *Battalion*, October 17, 1957, in College Station Publicity Notebook, vol. 2, p. 201.

68. "Group Asked to Aid in Cities' Growth," *Battalion*, March 26, 1958, in College Station Publicity Notebook, vol. 3, p. 22.

69. "City Council Approves Water Rate Increase," *Battalion*, April 29, 1958, in College Station Publicity Notebook, vol. 3, p. 29.

70. Minutes, vol. 4, April 28, 1958, p. 635.

71. *Ibid*, vol. 4, February 5, 1957 and April 27, 1959, pp. 597, 682; City of College Station, Minutes of Meeting of City Council, vol. 5, December 17, 1962, p. 787.

72. *Ibid*, vol. 5, March 25, 1963, p. 801.

73. *Ibid*, vol. 5, July 27, 1964, p. 849.

74. "Alderman Orr Will Run for Re-Election in CS," *Bryan Daily Eagle*, February 14, 1965, in College Station Publicity Notebook, vol. 2, p. 173.

75. Minutes, vol. 5, June 11, 1965, p. 884.

76. Welton Jones, "Dispute Rises Over Zoning at CS City Council Meeting," *Battalion*, February 26, 1957, in College Station Publicity Notebook, vol. 2, p. 173.

77. Minutes, vol. 5, March 16, 1961, p. 730; "City Dads Discuss Railroad Underpass," *Bryan Daily Eagle*, February 25, 1964, in College Station Publicity Notebook, vol. 5, p. 63.

78. "CS, Brazos in Dissent on Interchange Funds," *Bryan Daily Eagle*, July 28, 1964, in College Station Publicity Notebook, vol. 5, p. 106.

79. M. Rutherford, "Senator Herring May Force Delay in College Interchange," *Bryan Daily Eagle*, March 8, 1965, in College Station Publicity Notebook, vol. 5, p. 162.

80. "Interchange Land Ready," *Bryan Daily Eagle*, March 8, 1965, in College Station Publicity Notebook, vol. 5, p. 162.

81. Minutes, vol. 5, January 25, 1965 and February 4, 1965, pp. 860, 864.

82. *Ibid.*, vol. 5, January 24, 1966, p. 902.

83. Langford, *Remembrances*.

Chapter IV

1. Henry C. Dethloff, *A Centennial History of Texas A&M University*, 2 vols. (College Station, Texas: Texas A&M University, 1975), II, pp. 561, 568, 573 – 74.

2. *Ibid.*, II, p. 576.

3. D.A. Anderson, "Why the Need for a Federal Building and Its Location in the City of College Station," College Station, Texas, August 1, 1971, pp. 1 – 2 [Typescript.]

4. Jim Peters, "Population Hike Is Seen for CS," *Eagle*, undated newspaper clipping, in College Station Publicity Notebook, vol. 9, p. 66.

5. City of College Station, Minutes of Meeting of City Council, vol. 5, April 7, 1966, p. 908.

6. Elton R. Jones, "Anderson Picked Mayor in Close College Ballot," *Bryan Daily Eagle*, April 6, 1966, in College Station Publicity Notebook, vol. 6, p. 7.

7. Interview with David A. Anderson, September 22, 1983.

8. Kate Thomas, "Mayor Eyes Separate Chambers," *Daily Eagle*, March 29, 1970, in College Station Publicity Notebook, vol. 7, p. 164.

9. Interview with Anderson.

10. City of College Station, Minutes of Meeting of City Council, vol. 8, November 23, 1970, p. 1370.

11. *Ibid.*, vol. 8, October 21, 1970, p. 1360; D.A. Anderson, Memorandum to City Council and City Manager on Honorary Key, October 7, 1970, in City Hall Miscellaneous Files, College Station, Texas.

12. D.A. Anderson, Memorandum to City Council and City Manager on Sundry Items, May 4, 1970, in City Hall Miscellaneous Minutes, College Station, Texas.

13. Interview with Anderson.

14. Elton R. Jones, "College Station Five Year Plan Proposed," *Bryan Daily Eagle*, June 12, 1967, in College Station Publicity Notebook, vol. 6, p. 125.

15. D.A. Anderson, "Some Activities and Goals for City of College Station, Texas," College Station, Texas, October 1969, pp. 1 – 29. [Typescript.]; Interview with Anderson.

16. Minutes, vol. 8, April 27, 1970, pp. 1292 – 1299.

17. City of College Station, Minutes of Meeting of City Council, vol. 6, April 25, 1966, p. 914; Report of Annual Report Committee, May 12, 1970, in City Hall Miscellaneous Files, College Station, Texas.

18. Minutes, vol. 8, April 27, 1970, pp. 1292 – 1299.

19. Minutes, vol. 6, February 3, 1967, p. 978; Interview with Anderson.

20. *Ibid.*

21. *Ibid.*; Frank Griffis, "'House Breaking' in CS Signal Program Start," *Daily Eagle*, April 1, 1971, in College Station Publicity Notebook, vol. 8, p. 38.

22. "Lincoln School Blaze Displaces 100," *Bryan Daily Eagle*, January 21, 1966, in College Station Publicity Notebook, vol. 5, pp. 227 – 230.

23. Interview with Anderson.

24. *Ibid.*; City of College Station, Minutes of Meeting of City Council, vol. 7, June 24, 1968, p. 1082.

25. Joe Griska, "Lincoln Center Expands Fun," *Eagle*, August 5, 1973, in College Station Publicity Notebook, vol. 10, p. 47.

26. Minutes, vol. 6, April 5, 1967, p. 987.

27. Interview with Anderson; Interview with C.A. Bonnen, March 25, 1983.

28. Minutes, vol. 7, January 15, 1968, p. 1040.

29. *Ibid.*, vol. 7, April 3, 1968, p. 1063.

30. City of College Station, Minutes of Meeting of Planning and Zoning Commission, April 2, 1973 in City Hall Miscellaneous Files, College Station, Texas.

31. Minutes, vol. 7, October 31, 1968, p. 1104.

32. "CS Gets Grant for Water Plan," unidentified newspaper clipping, July 31, 1966, in College Station Publicity Notebook, vol. 6, p. 52.

33. Elton Jones, "CS Voters Okay Water Bond," *Bryan Daily Eagle*, September 18, 1966, in College Station Publicity Notebook, vol. 6, p. 74.

34. City of College Station, *Annual Report, 1968*, College Station, Texas, pp. 10 – 11.

35. Ran Boswell, City Manager of College Station, June 30, 1970, to Joe Sorrels, Director of Field Operations, Texas Water Quality Board in City Hall Miscellaneous Files, College Station, Texas; "College Station to Receive EDA $332,500 Grant," *Dallas Morning News*, May 1, 1970, in College Station Publicity Notebook, vol. 7, p. 180.

36. Minutes, vol. 7, July 24, 1967, pp. 1109 – 1012.

37. "College Station Breaks Ground for City Building," *Bryan Daily Eagle*, April 27, 1969, in College Station Publicity Notebook, vol. 7, p. 92.

38. Minutes, vol. 8, March 9, 1970, p. 1258.

39. *Annual Report, 1968*, p. 3.

40. Minutes, vol. 8, November 18, 1971, p. 1448.

41. Interview with Anderson.

42. D.A. Anderson, Memorandum to City Council and City Manager on Sundry Items, March 23, 1970, in City Hall Miscellaneous Files, College Station, Texas.

43. Lloyd L. James, "Notes on a Test Project Utilizing Ground Scrap Rubber Tires as a Stress Relieving Interface in the Rehabilitation of Pavements," College Station, Texas, September 17, 1970, pp. 1 – 5. [Typescript.]

44. *Ibid.*

45. Bob Stump, "Parks Readied for Summer," *Daily Eagle*, May 20, 1971, in College Station Publicity Notebook, vol. 8, p. 57.

46. Minutes, vol. 8, July 15, 1970, p. 1387.

105

47. *Ibid.*, vol. 8, March 23, 1970, p. 1271.

48. "Major Development Plans Outlined in CS," *Daily Eagle,* August 1969, in College Station Publicity Notebook, vol. 7, p. 124.

49. Minutes, vol. 7, August 25, 1969, pp. 1188 – 1191.

50. "City's Suit Delayed; Venue Change Denied," *Battalion,* September 9, 1970, in College Station Publicity Notebook, vol. 7, p. 199.

51. Interview with Anderson.

52. "CS Files Counter Suit Here," *Daily Eagle,* August 2, 1970, in College Station Publicity Notebook, vol. 7, p. 196.

53. Kate Thomas, "Judge Says He Will Decide CS Case in a Week," *Daily Eagle,* September 11, 1970, in College Station Publicity Notebook, vol. 7, p. 200.

54. *Ibid.*

55. Kate Thomas, "CS Wins Class Action Suit," *Daily Eagle,* September 23, 1970, in College Station Publicity Notebook, vol. 7, p. 207.

56. "Pat Callahan Wants Out of CS Lawsuit," *Daily Eagle,* October 5, 1970, in College Station Publicity Notebook, vol. 7, p. 207.

57. "Ruling Hits A&M Profs," *Dallas Morning News,* November 13, 1970, in College Station Publicity Notebook, vol. 8, p. 7.

58. Robert Ford, "Effects of CS Suit Widening," *Daily Eagle,* December 20, 1970, in College Station Publicity Notebook, vol. 8, p. 16.

59. D.A. Anderson, Mayor of College Station, November 30, 1970, to Dr. Jack K. Williams, President of Texas A&M University, in City Hall Miscellaneous Files, College Station, Texas.

60. Kate Thomas, "CS Class Action Suit Thrown Out," *Daily Eagle,* April 28, 1971, in College Station Publicity Notebook, vol. 8, p. 27.

61. Kate Thomas, "Prof Pay Ban Widened, Resignations Expected," *Daily Eagle,* April 28, 1971, in College Station Publicity Notebook, vol. 8, p. 47.

62. Minutes, vol. 8, May 5, 1971, p. 1411.

63. Kate Thomas, "Ryan and Ransdell Quit Council Post," *Daily Eagle,* May 6, 1971, in College Station Publicity Notebook, vol. 8, p. 53.

64. D.A. Anderson, Memorandum to Whom Addressed on Constitutional Amendment, State Employees, May 10, 1971, in City Hall Miscellaneous Files, College Station, Texas.

65. D.A. Anderson, Mayor of College Station, June 28, 1971, to Members of the College Station City Council, in City Hall Miscellaneous Files, College Station, Texas.

66. Minutes, vol. 8, November 4, 1971, p. 1439.

67. Interview with Anderson.

68. Frank Griffis, "Hervey Eyeing CS Unity Needs," *Daily Eagle,* August 2, 1971, in College Station Publicity Notebook, vol. 8, p. 74.

69. John Curylo, "Suit Filed by Student Over CS Elections," *Battalion,* November 23, 1971, in College Station Publicity Notebook, vol. 8, p. 109.

70. Minutes, vol. 8, December 17, 1971, pp. 1456 – 1457.

71. City of College Station, Minutes of Meeting of City Council, vol. 9, April 5, 1972, p. 1473.

72. *Ibid.*, vol. 9, July 24, 1972, p. 1493.

73. Dave Mayes, "There's 51,395 of Us, B-CS Probably SMSA," *Daily Eagle,* February 5, 1971, in College Station Publicity Notebook, vol. 8, p. 21.

74. Minutes, vol. 9, April 26, 1973, p. 1587.

75. Minutes, vol. 9, July 24, 1972, January 22, 1973, February 26, 1973, and April 23, 1973, pp. 1492, 1549, 1562, 1578.

76. "CS Swimming Pool Sets Unofficial Date," *Battalion,* October 4, 1974, in College Station Publicity Notebook, vol. 11, p. 130.

77. Connie Greenwall, "CS Okays 3 Per Cent Room Tax," *Eagle,* September 14, 1973, in College Station Publicity Notebook, vol. 10, p. 88.

78. "Pinnell Gets Pact," *Eagle,* November 11, 1972, in College Station Publicity Notebook, vol. 8, p. 164.

79. Jim Peters, "CS Looking at Its Future," *Eagle,* March 11, 1973, in College Station Publicity Notebook, vol. 9, p. 44.

80. "Residents Satisfied with CS," *Eagle,* April 20, 1973, in College Station Publicity Notebook, vol. 9, p. 70.

81. Connie Greenwell, "Romantic? — No, but Necessary," *Eagle,* May 19, 1973, in College Station Publicity Notebook, vol. 9, p. 116; Connie Greenwell, "Land Use Key Phase," *Eagle,* May 27, 1973, in College Station Publicity Notebook, vol. 9, p. 122.

82. Bobby Templeton, "City Plan Enters Phase II," *Eagle,* November 25, 1973, in College Station Publicity Notebook, vol. 10, p. 116; Minutes, vol. 9, January 24, 1974, p. 1659.

83. Minutes, vol. 9, October 23, 1972, p. 1532.

84. *Ibid.,* vol. 9, April 16, 1974, p. 1696.

85. Jamie Aitken, "City Adopts Master Plan," *Battalion,* September 10, 1976, in College Station Publicity Notebook, vol. 14, p. 59.

86. Bobby Templeton, "Getting Along with People Is the Trick," *Eagle,* December 2, 1973, in College Station Publicity Notebook, vol. 10, p. 113; Bobby Templeton, "Bardell Starts New Career," *Eagle,* December 15, 1973, in College Station Publicity Notebook, vol. 10, p. 130.

87. Minutes, vol. 9, December 14, 1973, p. 1656.

88. "Hervey Won't Run for CS Mayor," *Eagle,* February 19, 1974, in College Station Publicity Notebook, vol. 10, p. 148.

Chapter V

1. City of College Station, Minutes of Meeting of City Council, vol. 9, April 4, 1974, p. 1693.

2. Bobby Templeton, "Slim Margin Makes Holt New CS Mayor," *Eagle,* April 3, 1974, in College Station Publicity Notebook, vol. 11, p. 4.

3. City of College Station, Minutes of Meeting of City Council, vol. 10, May 15, 1975 and July 10, 1975, pp. 1808, 1826.

4. *Ibid.,* vol. 10, June 12, 1975, p. 1816.

5. "Water Well Dedicated by CS," *Eagle,* April 22, 1976, in College Station Publicity Notebook, vol. 13, p. 146.

6. O.M. Holt, Mayor of College Station, February 2, 1976, to Lloyd Joyce, Mayor of Bryan, in City Hall Miscellaneous Files, College Station, Texas.

7. June T. Bonarrigo, "Cities A-Buzz with Utility Talks," *Eagle*, January 27, 1976, in College Station Publicity Notebook, vol. 13, p. 40.

8. Lloyd Joyce, Mayor of Bryan, May 18, 1976, to Lorence Bravenec, Mayor of College Station, in City Hall Miscellaneous Files, College Station, Texas.

9. City of College Station, Minutes of Meeting of City Council, vol. 11, May 3, 1976 and June 30, 1976, pp. 1935, 1966.

10. Jerry Gray, "CS Council Inks Gulf States Pact After Election," *Eagle*, July 1, 1976, in College Station Publicity Notebook, vol. 14, p. 1.

11. "Bryan Bucks CS Plan for Water Development," *Eagle*, July 9, 1976, in College Station Publicity Notebook, vol. 14, p. 6.

12. Hank Wahrmund, "BVDC Approves College Station $1.2 Million Request," *Eagle*, August 13, 1976, in College Station Publicity Notebook, vol. 14, p. 32.

13. Public Utility Commission of Texas, Application of the City of Bryan for a Cease and Desist Order Against Gulf States Utilities Company, May 19, 1977, in City Hall Miscellaneous Files, College Station, Texas.

14. Jane M. Smith, "Sewer Construction to be Studied in CS," *Eagle*, September 22, 1977, in College Station Publicity Notebook, vol. 16, p. 20.

15. Jane M. Smith, "Bryan Proposes Cities Merge, but CS is Cool," *Eagle*, September 27, 1977, in College Station Publicity Notebook, vol. 16, p. 35.

16. *Ibid.*

17. Jane M. Smith, "College Station Experiences Capital Improvements Boom," *Eagle*, January 1, 1979, in College Station Publicity Notebook, vol. 18, p. 153.

18. Jane M. Smith, "Drilling Finished on CS Water Wells," *Eagle*, November 5, 1979, in College Station Publicity Notebook, vol. 20, p. 112.

19. David Crisp, "CS Dedicates Water System," *Eagle*, December 3, 1981, in College Station Publicity Notebook, vol. 25, p. 160.

20. Sam Logan, "TI Confirms Construction Plans for CS Plant; Size Not Revealed," *Eagle*, July 30, 1979, in College Station Publicity Notebook, vol. 19, p. 185.

21. "Regional Mall Announcement Good News for Whole Area," *Eagle*, June 7, 1979, in College Station Publicity Notebook, vol. 19, p. 112.

22. City of College Station, Minutes of Meeting of City Council, vol. 14, October 23, 1980, p. 3051.

23. Hazel Campbell, "Matching Funds to build new 45-Acre Bee Creek Park," *Battalion*, September 11, 1976, in College Station Publicity Notebook, vol. 11, p. 114.

24. Minutes, vol. 10, September 25, 1975, p. 1843.

25. Jerry Needham, "CS Council Passes Land Dedication Plans," *Battalion*, November 14, 1975, in College Station Publicity Notebook, vol. 13, p. 6.

26. Jerry Gray, "CS Sets Up Trust for City Park Donations," *Eagle*, July 9, 1976, in College Station Publicity Notebook, vol. 14, p. 7.

27. "College Station Opens Thomas Park Pool Today," *Eagle*, June 21, 1980, in College Station Publicity Notebook, vol. 22, p. 65.

28. "Choppers, Music to Fill Air at Park Dedication," *Eagle*, August 27, 1982, in College Station Publicity Notebook, vol. 26, p. 186.

29. "College Station Bike Paths to be Completed in Month," *Battalion*, August 4, 1976, in College Station Publicity Notebook, vol. 14, p. 25.

30. Jane M. Smith, "Scratch Bike Plan," *Eagle*, May 15, 1980, in College Station Publicity Notebook, vol. 22, p. 14.

31. City of College Station, Minutes of Meeting of City Council, vol. 12, February 9, 1978, p. 2389.

32. Kathy Ricketts, "An Artistic Look at College Station," *Eagle*, March 4, 1979, in College Station Publicity Notebook, vol. 19, p. 24.

33. Minutes, vol. 12, January 26, 1978, p. 2372.

34. Jane M. Smith, "CS Council Considering Consol Building Purchase," *Eagle*, August 9, 1979, in College Station Publicity Notebook, vol. 19, p. 198.

35. Rebecca Zimmerman, "CS Civic Center Recent Addition," *Battalion*, August 30, 1982, in College Station Publicity Notebook, vol. 26, p. 188.

36. Minutes, vol. 9, September 24, 1973, p. 1628.

37. Steve Gray, "Election System Sought," *Battalion*, February 11, 1976, in College Station Publicity Notebook, vol. 13, p. 58.

38. Minutes, vol. 10, April 5, 1976, and April 8, 1976, pp. 1911, 1917.

39. *Ibid.*, vol. 10, April 27, 1976, p. 1931.

40. Jerry Needham, "CS Voters Pass All 9 Bond Issues," *Battalion*, June 30, 1976, in College Station Publicity Notebook, vol. 13, p. 204.

41. Jerry Gray, "Ward System Vote Upheld," *Eagle*, October 22, 1976, in College Station Publicity Notebook, vol. 14, p. 90.

42. Jamie Aitken, "Intervention Suit Filed," *Battalion*, September 8, 1976, in College Station Publicity Notebook, vol. 14, p. 56.

43. Gray, "Ward system," vol. 14, p. 90.

44. Minutes, vol. 12, April 3, 1978, p. 2423.

45. Frank May, "No Opposition to Industry Voiced," *Eagle*, December 18, 1980, in College Station Publicity Notebook, vol. 23, p. 92.

46. Frank May, "Planners Pave Way for Industry," *Eagle*, December 19, 1980, in College Station Publicity Notebook, vol. 23, p. 94.

47. Frank May, "Residents Meet to Plan Strategy," *Eagle*, December 19, 1980, in College Station Publicity Notebook, vol. 23, p. 100.

48. Frank May, "College Station Mayor Defends Decision," *Eagle*, January 9, 1981, in College Station Publicity Notebook, vol. 23, p. 105.

49. Frank May, "Raintree Group Begins Recall," *Eagle*, January 11, 1981, in College Station Publicity Notebook, vol. 23, p. 106.

50. Frank May, "Industry Discloses Its Identity," *Eagle*, January 14, 1981, in College Station Publicity Notebook, vol. 23, p. 107.

51. Frank May, "Westinghouse to Buy Land," *Eagle*, January 22, 1981, in College Station Publicity Notebook, vol. 23, p. 116.

52. Frank May, "Westinghouse Eyes Option to Buy Land," *Eagle*, January 11, 1981, in College Station Publicity Notebook, vol. 23, p. 110.

53. Frank May, "Referendum Non-Binding, Says Attorney," *Eagle*, January 30, 1981, in College Station Publicity Notebook, vol. 23, p. 113.

54. Belinda McCoy, "Residents to File Petition Today," *Battalion*, January 28, 1981, in College Station Publicity Notebook, vol. 23, p. 123.

55. Frank May, "Council Denies Raintree Petition," *Eagle*, February 27, 1981, in College Station Publicity Notebook, vol. 24, p. 40.

56. Belinda McCoy, "Raintree Residents to File Suit," *Battalion*, March 4, 1981, in College Station Publicity Notebook, vol. 24, p. 40.

57. Frank May, "Public to Speak on Rezoning," *Eagle*, February 25, 1981, in College Station Publicity Notebook, vol. 24, p. 33; Frank May, "Westinghouse Buys Disputed Site," *Eagle*, March 4, 1981, in College Station Publicity Notebook, vol. 24, p. 54.

58. May, "Public to Speak," vol. 24, p. 33.

59. Frank May, "Survey Added to College Station Ballot," *Eagle*, March 12, 1981, in College Station Publicity Notebook, vol. 24, p. 72.

60. Frank May, "Voters Pick Ringer, Jones, Prause," *Eagle*, April 5, 1981, in College Station Publicity Notebook, vol. 24, p. 124.

61. Frank May, "Raintree Residents Call it Quits in Squabble," *Eagle*, May 2, 1981, in College Station Publicity Notebook, vol. 24, p. 145.

62. Jane Mills Smith, "College Station Citizens Prepare to Revise Comprehensive Plan," *Eagle*, October 7, 1979, in College Station Publicity Notebook, vol. 20, p. 79.

63. Frank May, "Updated CS Comprehensive Plan Ready," *Eagle*, January 30, 1981, in College Station Publicity Notebook, vol. 23, p. 126.

64. City of College Station, Minutes of Meeting of College Station, vol. 15, July 23, 1981, p. 3286.

65. *Ibid.*, vol. 15, July 9, 1981, p. 3269.

66. Frank May, "Land Buy Called a Low-Risk Opportunity," *Eagle*, July 11, 1981, in College Station Publicity Notebook, vol. 25, p. 23.

67. *Ibid.*

68. Frank May, "Spearman Swings CS Land Purchase," *Eagle*, July 24, 1981, in College Station Publicity Notebook, vol. 25, p. 40.

69. Frank May, "College Station Completes Purchase of Land," *Eagle*, July 24, 1981, College Station Publicity Notebook, vol. 25, p. 42.

70. David Crisp, "CS Industrial Park May be Just What Texas is Looking For," *Eagle*, December 21, 1981, in College Station Publicity Notebook, vol. 25, p. 171.

71. May, "College Station Completes Purchase," p. 42.

72. Davis Crisp, "CS Officials Advance Plans for Industrial Park," *Eagle*, April 14, 1982, in College Station Publicity Notebook, vol. 26, p. 84.

73. David Crisp, "Commission Hearing on Plan 2000 Today," *Eagle*, June 17, 1982, in College Station Publicity Notebook, vol. 26, p. 129

74. David Crisp, "Future Growth Outlined in Plan 2000," *Eagle*, June 22, 1982, in College Station Publicity Notebook, vol. 26, p. 134

College Station Mayors & Councilmen Since Incorporation

1938
Mayor John H. Binney
Letcher P. Gabbard
Luther G. Jones
Ernest K. Langford
Alva Mitchell
George B. Wilcox

1939
Mayor John H. Binney
Letcher P. Gabbard
Luther G. Jones
Samuel A. Lipscomb
Wayne E. Long (resigned 9/39)
Joseph A. Orr (replaced Long 10/39)
George B. Wilcox

1940
Mayor Frank G. Anderson
Ernest K. Langford
Samuel A. Lipscomb
Thurmond A. Munson
Joseph A. Orr
George B. Wilcox

1941
Mayor Frank G. Anderson
Ernest K. Langford
Samuel A. Lipscomb
Thurmond A. Munson
Joseph A. Orr
George B. Wilcox

1942
Ward System First Instated
Mayor Ernest K. Langford
Ward I   Joseph A. Orr
         George B. Wilcox
Ward II Patton W. Burns
         Thurmond A. Munson
Ward III Walter D. Lloyd (resigned 11/42)
         Lloyd Smith (resigned 11/42)

1943
Mayor Ernest K. Langford
Ward I   Joseph A. Orr
         George B. Wilcox
Ward II Charles W. Crawford
         Marion T. Harrington
Ward III Ewing E. Brown
         Robert L. Brown

1944
Mayor Ernest K. Langford
Ward I   Joseph A. Orr
         George B. Wilcox
Ward II Charles W. Crawford
         Marion T. Harrington
Ward III Ewing E. Brown
         Robert L. Brown

1945
Mayor Ernest K. Langford
Ward I   Joseph A. Orr
         George B. Wilcox
Ward II Charles W. Crawford
         Marion T. Harrington
Ward III Ewing E. Brown
         Robert L. Brown

1946
Mayor Ernest K. Langford
Ward I   Joseph A. Orr
         George B. Wilcox
Ward II Charles W. Crawford
         Marion T. Harrington
Ward III E.E. Ames
         Robert L. Brown

1947
Mayor Ernest K. Langford
Ward I   W. Howard Badgett
         Joseph A. Orr
Ward II Grady W. Black
         Marion T. Harrington
Ward III E.E. Ames
         Frank B. Brown, Jr.

1948
Mayor Ernest K. Langford
Ward I   W. Howard Badgett
         Joseph A. Orr
Ward II Grady W. Black
         Robert B. Halpin
Ward III E.E. Ames
         Frank B. Brown, Jr.

1949
Mayor Ernest K. Langford
Ward I   W. Howard Badgett
         Joseph A. Orr
Ward II Grady W. Black
         Robert B. Halpin
Ward III E.E. Ames
         Ewing E. Brown (resigned 6/49)
         William D. Fitch (replaced Brown 7/49)

1950
Mayor Ernest K. Langford
Ward I   W. Howard Badgett
         Joseph A. Orr
Ward II Grady W. Black
         Robert B. Halpin
Ward III E.E. Ames
         William D. Fitch

1951
Mayor Ernest K. Langford
Ward I   W. Howard Badgett
         Joseph A. Orr
Ward II Harry L. Boyer
         Robert B. Halpin
Ward III E.E. Ames (resigned 7/51)
         Alton P. Boyett (replaced Ames 7/51)
         William D. Fitch

1952
Mayor Ernest K. Langford
Ward I   W. Howard Badgett
         Marion Pugh
Ward II Harry L. Boyer
         Joseph H. Sorrels
Ward III Alton P. Boyett
         William D. Fitch

1953
Mayor Ernest K. Langford
Ward I   Joseph A. Orr
         Marion Pugh

Ward II Grady W. Black
        Joseph H. Sorrels
Ward III Alton P. Boyett
         Ernest Seeger

1954
Mayor Ernest K. Langford
Ward I Joseph A. Orr
       Marion Pugh
Ward II Grady W. Black
        Joseph H. Sorrels
Ward III Alton P. Boyett
         Ernest Seeger

1955
Mayor Ernest K. Langford
Ward I Joseph A. Orr
       Marion Pugh
Ward II Grady W. Black
        Joseph H. Sorrels
Ward III Alton P. Boyett
         Ernest Seeger

1956
Mayor Ernest K. Langford
Ward I Joseph A. Orr
       Marion Pugh
Ward II Grady W. Black
        Joseph H. Sorrels
Ward III Alton P. Boyett
         Ernest Seeger

1957
Mayor Ernest K. Langford
Ward I Joseph A. Orr
       Marion Pugh
Ward II David A. Anderson
        Joseph H. Sorrels
Ward III Alton P. Boyett
         L. J. McCall

1958
Mayor Ernest K. Langford
Ward I Carl W. Landiss
       Joseph A. Orr
Ward II David A. Anderson
        Joseph H. Sorrels
Ward III Alton P. Boyett
         L. J. McCall

1959
Mayor Ernest K. Langford

Ward I Carl W. Landiss
       Joseph A. Orr
Ward II David A. Anderson
        Joseph H. Boyett
Ward III Alton P. Boyett
         William A. Smith

1960
Mayor Ernest K. Langford
Ward I Carl W. Landiss
       Joseph A. Orr
Ward II David A. Anderson
        Joseph H. Sorrels
Ward III Alton P. Boyett
         William A. Smith

1961
Mayor Ernest K. Langford
Ward I Carl W. Landiss
       Joseph A. Orr
Ward II David A. Anderson
        Joseph H. Sorrels
Ward III Alton P. Boyett
         Antone Rosprim

1962
Mayor Ernest K. Langford
Ward I Carl W. Landiss
       Joseph A. Orr
Ward II David A. Anderson
        Joseph H. Sorrels
Ward III Alton P. Boyett
         Antone Rosprim

1963
Mayor Ernest K. Langford
Ward I Carl W. Landiss
       Joseph A. Orr
Ward II Robert R. Rhodes
        Joseph H. Sorrels
Ward III Alton P. Boyett
         Antone Rosprim

1964
Mayor Ernest K. Langford
Ward I Theo R. Holleman
       Joseph A. Orr
Ward II Oris M. Holt
        Robert R. Rhodes
Ward III Alton P. Boyett
         Antone Rosprim

1965

Mayor Ernest K. Langford
Ward I Theo R. Holleman
       Joseph A. Orr
Ward II Oris M. Holt
        Robert R. Rhodes
Ward III Alton P. Boyett
         Antone Rosprim

1966
Mayor David A. Anderson
Ward I Homer Adams
       Joseph A. Orr (resigned 3/66)
       Bill J. Cooley (replaced Orr 5/66)
Ward II Oris M. Holt
        Robert R. Rhodes
Ward III Alton P. Boyett
         Antone Rosprim

1967
Mayor David A. Anderson
Ward I Homer Adams
       Bill J. Cooley
Ward II Oris M. Holt
        Robert R. Rhodes
Ward III Alton P. Boyett
         Antone Rosprim

1968
Place System Instated
Mayor David A. Anderson
Ward I Bill J. Cooley
Ward II Robert R. Rhodes
Ward III Antone Rosprim (resigned 5/68)
         Dan R. Davis (replaced Rosprim 5/68)

Place II James H. Dozier
Place IV Oris M. Holt
Place VI Theo R. Holleman (died 10/68)
         Clifford H. Ransdell (replaced Holleman 12/68)

1969
Mayor David A. Anderson
Place I Bill J. Cooley
Place II James H. Dozier
Place III Joseph J. McGraw
Place IV Oris M. Holt
Place V Dan R. Davis
Place VI Clifford H. Ransdell

1970
Mayor David A. Anderson

110

Place I Bill J. Cooley
Place II James H. Dozier
Place III Joseph J. McGraw
Place IV Cecil B. Ryan
Place V Dan R. Davis
Place VI Clifford H. Ransdell

1971
Mayor David A. Anderson (resigned 6/71)
Fred Brison (Interim mayor 6/71 - 8/71)
James B. Hervey (replaced Anderson 8/71)
Place I Fred Brison
Place II James H. Dozier (resigned 11/71)
Homer B. Adams (replaced Dozier 12/71)
Place III Don Dale
Place IV Cecil B. Ryan (resigned 5/71)
James D. Lindsay (replaced Ryan 6/71)
Place V Rudolph Radeleff
Place VI Clifford H. Ransdell (resigned 5/71)
Clarence A. Bonnen (replaced Ransdell 6/71)

1972
Mayor James B. Hervey
Place I Fred Brison
Place II Homer B. Adams
Place III Don Dale
Place IV James D. Lindsay
Place V Rudolph Radeleff
Place VI C.A. Bonnen

1973
Mayor James B. Hervey
Place I Fred Brison
Place II Homer B. Adams
Place III Don Dale
Place IV James D. Lindsay
Place V Rudolph Radeleff (died 1/74)
Place VI C.A. Bonnen

1974
Mayor Oris M. Holt
Place I Fred Brison
Place II Homer B. Adams
Place III Don Dale
Place IV James Gardner

Place V Lorence Bravenec
Place VI James H. Dozier

1975
Mayor Oris M. Holt
Place I Gary Halter
Place II Homer B. Adams
Place III Bob Bell
Place IV James Gardner
Place V Lorence Bravenec
Place VI James H. Dozier

1976
Mayor Lorence Bravenec
Place I Gary Halter
Place II Lane Stephenson
Place III Larry Ringer
Place IV James Gardner
Place V Anne Hazen
Place VI James H. Dozier

1977
Ward (District) System Re-instated
Mayor Lorence Bravenec
District I Gary Halter
District II Lane Stephenson
District III Larry Ringer
District IV James Gardner
District V Anne Hazen
District VI James H. Dozier

1978
Mayor Lorence Bravenec
District I Gary Halter
District II Homer B. Adams
District III Larry Ringer
District IV Patricia Boughton
District V Anne Hazen
District VI James H. Dozier

1979
Place System Re-instated
Mayor Lorence Bravenec
Place I Gary Halter
District II Homer B. Adams
Place III Larry Ringer
District IV Patricia Boughton
Place V Tony Jones
District VI James H. Dozier

1980
Mayor Gary Halter
Place I Roy Kelly
Place II Robert Runnels
Place III Larry Ringer
Place IV Patricia Boughton
Place V Tony Jones
Place VI James H. Dozier

1981
Mayor Gary Halter
Place I Alvin H. Prause
Place II Robert Runnels
Place III Larry Ringer
Place IV Patricia Boughton
Place V Tony Jones
Place VI James H. Dozier

1982
Mayor Gary Halter
Place I Alvin H. Prause
Place II Robert Runnels
Place III Larry Ringer
Place IV Patricia Boughton
Place V Tony Jones
Place VI Lynn Nemec

1983
Mayor Gary Halter
Place I Alvin H. Prause
Place II Robert Runnels
Place III Vicky Reinke
Place IV Patricia Boughton
Place V Gary Anderson
Place VI Lynn Nemec-McIlhaney

1984
Mayor Gary Halter
Place I Alvin H. Prause
Place II Robert Runnels
Place III Vicky Reinke
Place IV Patricia Boughton
Place V Gary Anderson
Place VI Lynn Nemec-McIlhaney

1985
Mayor Gary Halter
Place I Fred Brown
Place II Dr. Robert C. Runnels
Place III Theresa (Terri) Tongco
Place IV Patricia (Pat) Boughton
Place V James B. Bond
Place VI Lynn McIlhaney

1986
Mayor Larry J. Ringer
Place   I   Fred Brown
Place   II   Sara Goode Jones
Place   III Theresa (Terri) Tongco
Place   IV   Patricia (Pat) Boughton
Place   V   James B. Bond
Place   VI   Dick Haddox

1987
Mayor Larry J. Ringer
Place   I   Fred Brown
Place   II   Sara Goode Jones
Place   III Lynn McIlhaney
Place   IV   Patricia Boughton
Place   V   Jim Gardner
Place   VI   Dick Haddox

(Appointed Officials)
William K. Cole, City Manager
Cathy Locke, City Attorney
Dian Jones, City Secretary
Philip Banks, City Judge
David Fetzer, Financial Advisor

112

www.ingramcontent.com/pod-product-compliance
Lightning Source LLC
Chambersburg PA
CBHW062104090426
42741CB00015B/3331